W0017378

FINDING OUR FOUNDATION

Let us be silent that we
may hear the whisper of God

FINDING OUR FOUNDATION

by

CAROL ANN GRAY

A History of Plumstead Friends Meeting

All photographs were taken by Carol Ann Gray unless noted otherwise.

ISBN 978-1-66783-324-8

Cover photo- photo by Dafydd Jones
Back Cover- work day at Plumstead in 2010
Frontispiece- entry door to the Plumstead Meetinghouse

TABLE OF CONTENTS

PREFACE

The Plumstead Friends Meetinghouse, located in Bucks County, Pennsylvania, is a small, one-story rectangular stone and stucco building set back from Point Pleasant Pike. It is nestled among stately trees over one hundred years old, and even from the road, there is a quiet air of antiquity about it.

The building's interior contains just one room, filled with mismatched, handmade wooden benches, some scarred with graffiti carved by Quaker children over a century ago. The windows have old wavy glass panes, and the wainscoting on the walls is a muted gray. There are runners, woven by hand, on the otherwise bare wooden floor. There is neither plumbing nor electricity, and heat is provided by a wood-burning stove.

For at least half the year, the exterior doors remain open during Meeting for Worship, allowing the breeze and the sounds of birds, insects, and passing traffic to enter. In winter, the blaze from a crackling fire gives a snug sense of comfort. There is a quiet reverence in the morning sunlight streaming through the windows, a sense of authenticity in this building made from natural materials shaped by human hands. There is a groundedness in the past as we connect in the present with the loving Source of creation, life, and joy.

I have been a member of Plumstead Friends Meeting since its earliest days as a monthly meeting some twenty years ago. Questions about the meetinghouse, however, nagged at me from the very beginning. Why was the meetinghouse facing away from the road (appearing rather unwelcoming)? There had been a school and a previous meetinghouse made of logs on the property—where had they been located? It was said that wounded soldiers from the Battle of Germantown were brought to Plumstead for recovery—how did they happen to arrive at the building of a pacifist congregation in such a remote location? The stone meetinghouse was built in 1752, and was rebuilt in 1875—was it a restoration or had changes been made?

The catalyst for me to find the answers to these questions occurred in 2019, when the meetinghouse floor was replaced, revealing in the exposed crawlspace the colonial foundation walls and the remnants of two previously hidden fireplaces. The echoes of the past had now turned into a tangible puzzle begging to be solved.

Although essays and booklets had been prepared about Plumstead Friends Meeting, nothing comprehensive had ever been written about its history. Unfortunately, none of the minutes from Plumstead Preparative Meeting had been preserved, [1] but the minutes from Buckingham Monthly Meeting, to which Plumstead reported, were available at the Friends Historical Library and online at *ancestry.com*. Much of my research, therefore, involved reading thousands of pages

---

[1] Miriam Broadhurst (1894–1988) stated that Wesley Haldeman, who was the editor of the Newtown Enterprise, was a member of Plumstead Meeting when it was laid down. Haldeman at times went alone to the meetinghouse, built a fire, and sat down. Miriam attended Meeting with him one First Day, and he expressed to her how mad he was about the laying down of the Meeting. He was said to have burned the minute book, but fortunately the treasurer, Comly Michener, retained the financial records. These were passed down to his grandson of the same name.

of minutes from Buckingham Monthly Meeting, Bucks Quarterly Meeting, and Philadelphia Yearly Meeting, as well as the diary of John Dyer and other contemporaneous works. Immersing myself in the culture and theology of our Quaker roots became a deeply rewarding and enriching experience for me. I was moved to learn of the early hardships caused by accidents, fire, and disease that colonial Friends suffered, and I was surprised to learn of the persecution and even imprisonment of Quakers at the hands of their neighbors during the Revolutionary War. During those years, simply gathering at the Plumstead Meetinghouse each First Day at the appointed hour was an act of great courage. It was inspiring to see that during the bitter Schism of the 1800s, Friends were still opening their hearts to the welfare of the oppressed, such as slaves and indigenous peoples. And along the way, I discovered the answers to most of my questions.

The exposed crawlspace, foundation, and fireplace. Photo by Bill Hoblin

For the sake of clarity, I have tried to keep dates and nomenclature as consistent as possible. So, for example, for dates prior to the adoption of the Gregorian calendar, I have expressed (in the narrative) the eleventh month of 1719 in its modern form, January 1720. I have kept the name of the Delaware River as such throughout, although it had other names before the arrival of the English colonists. In Chapter One I have, at times, referred to the Lenape as "Indians," which, although inaccurate, is a term they do not object to. Three of the chapters, "Europeans Arrive in the Delaware Valley," "The State of the Church," and "Changes in Quaker Culture and Theology," do not deal directly with Plumstead Meeting, but instead provide a context designed to make the chapter which follows it more meaningful.

I would like to thank Jordan Landes of the Friends Historical Library, as well as the librarians and staff of the Bucks County Historical Society/Mercer Museum, for all their assistance. The staff of the Recorder of Deeds Office at the Doylestown Court House kindly did the complicated title search of the property for me. I am indebted to Curtis Zunigha of the Delaware Tribe of Oklahoma for reviewing the first chapter of this book, and to historian Seth B. Hinshaw for his ideas about the design of the 1752 Plumstead Meetinghouse. My daughter-in-law, Whitley Gray, created many of the maps appearing in the book, and local historian Jesse Crooks provided helpful information concerning the Plumstead burial ground. Plumstead Friends Meeting members, in particular Jonathan Trueblood, Beth Taylor, Bill Hoblin, Harry Branson, Carol Ann Hey, and Dafydd Jones contributed information, photographs, ideas, and support. My special thanks to my husband, Alan D. Gray, for the time he spent in technical assistance (such as measuring buildings, making scans, and fixing computers), for photographs he contributed, and for his patience and encouragement with this project.

LAND ACKNOWLEDGEMENT

We, the members of Plumstead Friends Meeting, acknowledge that our meetinghouse is situated on the ancestral lands of the Lenape, a territory that saw thousands of years of rich indigenous history before the arrival of William Penn. As we honor those First Peoples, we remind ourselves to continue their attitude of respect for this land, and to nurture a sacred relationship to it.

Drawing by Herbert and John Kraft, used by permission of the Delaware Tribe of Indians, Oklahoma

CHAPTER ONE:

EUROPEANS ARRIVE IN THE DELAWARE VALLEY

THE DELAWARE VALLEY BEFORE PENN[2]

The Native Americans of the Delaware Valley, the Lenape, were a people who, at first contact, controlled a territory extending from southern New York through New Jersey, eastern Pennsylvania, and into present day Delaware. The Lenape sociopolitical structure was egalitarian and democratic. They had generally peaceful relations with the Powhatans to the south, the Susquehannocks to the west, and the Iroquois to the north, and were noted for their skill in diplomacy and mediation.[3]

---

[2] Most of this section is based on Soderlund's *Lenape Country* unless otherwise noted

[3] The Delaware River was their Main Street for travel and trade, pulling together Lenape country. Its tributaries led to dispersed residential villages, where the forest was cleared for agriculture. In spring, women planted corn, tobacco, beans, squash, and gourds. In summer and early autumn, the Lenape hunted and fished, tended and harvested the crops, and preserved food for winter. The land was held cooperatively, by the community as whole, not by individuals. The Lenape religion was closely connected with the natural world and with their homeland. The land held the highest possible meaning, and contained sacred sites that were integral to the practices of religion and the well-being of the tribal culture.

Estimates as to the number of Lenape pre-contact vary widely. When Giovanni da Verrazzano explored the coastline north of the Carolinas, he reported that it was densely populated everywhere and "smoky with Indian bonfires." [4]Verrazzano first met the Lenape off Sandy Hook, New Jersey, in 1524. During subsequent years, European fishermen, whalers, and slavers interacted with native peoples on the coast.[5] Dutch explorers, who had previously claimed the territory from New England to Virginia, entered the Delaware River about 1615 and established a trading post across the river from present day Philadelphia. The Dutch name for the major tributary in that area, the Schuylkill, remains to this day. The Lenape welcomed the opportunity for trade and enthusiastically added woolens, firearms, and metal implements to their culture.

In 1631, after negotiating with the Lenape for land, the Dutch began building a plantation colony at Swanendael, near present day Lewes, Delaware. The Lenape expected Swanendael to be only a trading station. Aware of the abuses the Powhatans suffered at Jamestown, the Lenape refused to tolerate the establishment of plantations, and within a year they massacred the entire settlement.[6] After the conflict,

[4] Mann, p. 50. Travelers to New England c. 1600 reported that the area was thickly settled and well defended. In 1603, Samuel de Champlain abandoned his idea of establishing a base on Cape Cod for this reason.

[5] Due to this contact, indigenous people were succumbing to diseases such as smallpox, measles, and influenza even before the first trading posts were established in the Delaware Valley. Meanwhile, the French had penetrated deep into Canada, infecting the Hurons, who brought contagious disease to their trading partners, the Susquehannocks, who then in turn infected the Lenape.

[6] The Dutch built a dormitory, cookhouse, and palisades, and the twenty-eight colonists then sent for additional men and supplies. There appear to be multiple conflicts and misunderstandings leading to the attack, not the least of which was the awareness by the Lenape of what was happening to the Powhatans. There was creeping land encroachment in Jamestown; domestic animals, vital to the success of the colony, were allowed to roam free and to damage Powhatan crops. The English

however, the Lenape quickly focused on re-establishing good relations and trade with the Dutch, having proven their supremacy and willingness to use violence if provoked. The Swanendael massacre delayed expansive agriculture in the region for decades, but it also prevented much of the brutality endured in other colonies.

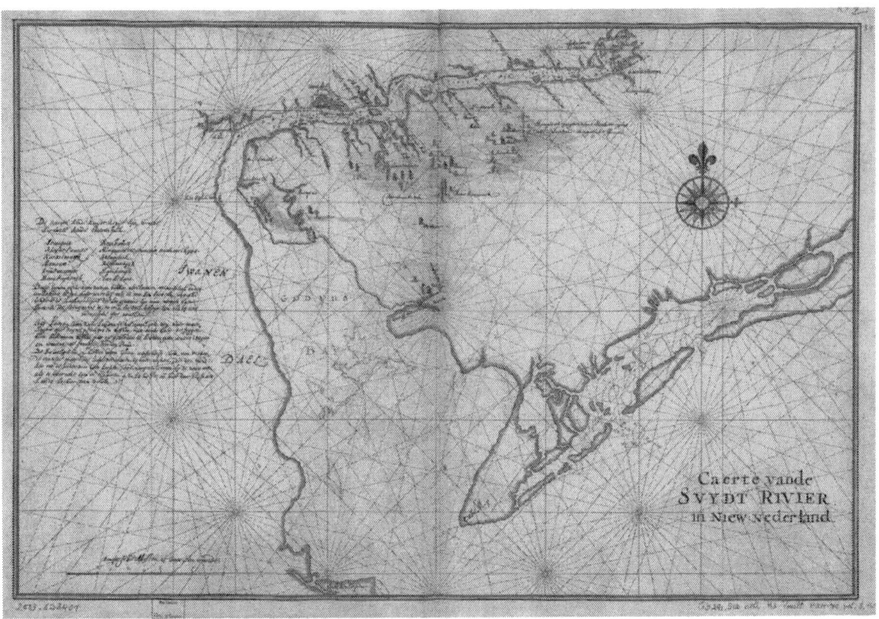

A Dutch map dated 1639 showing the Delaware River area, Lenape villages, and the area of Swanendael

prioritized growing the more lucrative tobacco over food crops, then stole food from the native peoples. During this period, the appearance of European traders also precipitated a ten-year war between the Lenape and the Susquehannocks. There was fierce competition for European goods, already in inadequate supply, and the Lenape wanted to monopolize the fur trade in their territory. This was part of a larger struggle all over North America for control of the Atlantic fur trade. The resolution of the Lenape/Susquehannock war created a strong alliance that served both tribes well during subsequent conflicts with the Iroquois and the English

Just a few years later, the Swedes established themselves on the Delaware. They knew this area had been claimed and settled by the Dutch; however, they also knew the Dutch were focused on New Amsterdam to the north. Peter Minuit, a Dutchman who was backed by the Swedish government, founded a Swedish colony in 1638 near present day Wilmington. [7]

As decades passed, the Lenape and Europeans established a framework of interaction based on mutual values and self-determination, shared use of land, and an inclusive definition of freedom, all facilitated by a mutual commitment to economic gain.

In 1654, a Swedish engineer, Peter Lindestrom, surveyed and mapped the Delaware River. He reported that in the area of present day Philadelphia, there were four Lenape villages on the Delaware River and two on the Schuylkill.[8] These villages were strategically located to take advantage of the fur trade between the Susquehannocks, Dutch, and Swedes. The Lenape also grew corn at the villages on a large scale as a cash crop. Lindstrom reported, "This is occupied in the greatest force by the most intelligent [of several Lenape groups] who own this river and dwell here. There they have their dwellings side by side one another and have cleared and cultivated [their land] with great power."[i] Each settlement was "several hundred men strong." By this time, the Swedes had created a permanent settlement (and capital of New Sweden) just south of the area at Tinicum, while the Dutch still had their trading post on the east bank of the Delaware River called Fort Nassau. From this confluence of Lenape, Swedes and

---

[7] Sweden at that time was three times its current size, a great military power that sought to extend its influence into the New World. It included what is now modern-day Sweden, as well as parts of Finland, Norway, Estonia, and Germany.

[8] one of these, Passyunk, was located in the current Philadelphia neighborhood of the same name.

Dutch, foot trails radiated out in all directions, connecting to other peoples. Although now declining in population from one of many epidemics, the Lenape still outnumbered the Europeans by a factor of 10. In the 1654 Treaty of Tinicum, the Lenape sachem Mattahorn issued a stern reminder that the Europeans lived in Lenape country and traded there only with Lenape permission. Compensation was expected when treaties were signed, he said, and the Europeans needed to fulfill their contractual obligations.

The next twenty-five years brought continued changes: a Lenape war with the Iroquois over the fur trade; a war between the Dutch and the English that resulted in the Delaware Valley becoming an English colony; additional onslaughts of disease that caused precipitous declines in the native population.

The balance of power was now shifting in a more permanent way, as English settlers migrated into Pennsylvania from other colonies. The Lenape, familiar with the English record elsewhere, reacted to the takeover and killed more than ten English and allies. The reasons were many: death of Lenape family members, encroachment on their land, the refusal of the English to meet with them to talk. In 1670, the Lenape still outnumbered the Europeans by 3 to 1, and they could have destroyed the English settlements from New York to New Castle if they had been organized and fortified by allies. However, the reality was that the English now controlled all the colonies on the east coast, and if the Lenape went to full scale war with them, the native peoples had no source of gunpowder or lead.

For a period of 150 years following the onset of European contact the Lenape natives successfully prevented the very plantation system that William Penn was about to establish. At the time of Penn's arrival, there were Dutch and Swedish forts and settlers along the Delaware River, and Lenape villages with trade routes to the interior. It was a dynamic, tolerant, multinational society, accustomed to resolving conflicts with negotiations rather than war, a society that would greatly impact the Quaker settlers who were soon to arrive.

QUAKER BEGINNINGS IN ENGLAND

The Religious Society of Friends arose in England in the middle of the seventeenth century, a time of turbulence and change in both religion and politics. In the established Church of England, great emphasis was placed upon outward ceremony; there, and in such dissenting churches as the Baptists and Presbyterians, religious faith was also generally identified with the authority of the Bible or the acceptance of a formal creed. Many individuals, however, became increasingly dissatisfied with ceremonies and creeds, and broke away from these churches. Singly or in small groups, they turned inward in search of a religion of personal experience and direct communion with God.

George Fox (1624–1691) was one of these seekers. While many religious dissenters who welcomed Fox's message of direct communion and continuing revelation became Friends, those persons who were committed to the Church of England or to other churches regarded his message as unwelcome, heretical, and treasonous. It was unwelcome, since Fox and some of his followers often invaded and disrupted the church services of others. It was heretical, since the idea of continuing revelation displaced the church and even the Scriptures as finally authoritative. It was treasonous, since those who embraced this idea also refused to acknowledge the authority of the state (with its established church) as taking precedence over the authority of individual conscience, consequently refusing to take any oath of allegiance to the state or to pay tithes towards the maintenance of the Anglican Church. Accordingly, the meetings of early Quakers were frequently disrupted by angry mobs, their meetinghouses were vandalized and burned, and they were themselves subjected to imprisonment and cruel treatment by officials of the state. Yet, like the early Christian church, the Quaker movement gained more adherents despite—or because of—the persecution.

This combination of persecution and expansion yielded several important consequences. First, the Quakers' sense of themselves as a distinct people with a divine mission became stronger. Unlike other dissenters, they insisted on holding their meetings publicly in spite of persecution, and thus began earning their reputation for scrupulous honesty. Secondly, they published numerous books and articles intended to explain and justify Quaker principles, including the defense of a woman's right to preach and prophesy. Third, the early Friends realized that their movement required at least some kind of institutional structure: not only to provide material assistance and emotional support for those being persecuted but also to nurture and discipline the individual and group life of its adherents. Thus was initiated, at Fox's urging, the bottom-up system of monthly, quarterly, and yearly meetings. [ii]

WILLIAM PENN AND THE HOLY EXPERIMENT

William Penn (1644–1718) came from a family of the upper gentry, with personal ties at court, and income largely from tenanted land. At the age of twenty-two, Penn joined the Society of Friends and often traveled with George Fox. Penn published many pamphlets in defense of Quakerism and in 1668, he was imprisoned in the Tower of London for the crime of blasphemy. There, he was placed in solitary confinement in an unheated cell and threatened with a life sentence. Penn was finally released after eight months of incarceration.

Image licensed by Vectorstock

William Penn's father, Admiral William Penn (1621–1670), then wrote to the Duke of York to secure his son's protection. The Duke and the King of England, in honor of the Admiral's lifetime services to the Crown, promised to protect young Penn and make him a royal counselor. Over the next decade, as Quaker persecutions continued, the younger Penn decided to appeal directly to the King and the Duke, and proposed a solution: a mass emigration of Quakers to North America. The Crown owed a debt to the now deceased Admiral Penn of £16,000; it also had won all the Dutch possessions in North America in 1664. The establishment of a Quaker colony neatly discharged the Crown's debt, removing a group that was a clear threat to the English social order; for Penn it secured the possibility of making profits from the sale of land, and for fellow Quakers it guaranteed safety from religious persecution. It also provided a way for rural Quaker householders to own their own farms and to practice Quaker values without being either traditionally poor or excessively commercial. The King granted a charter of 45,000 square miles to Penn in 1681. The following year, between August 1682 and October of that year, twenty-three ships arrived from England carrying two thousand settlers, including William Penn aboard the *Wellcome*. Another twenty-one ships arrived in 1683, doubling the colonial English population within a year.

The Wellcome lands in Pennsylvania. Image used with permission of the Historical Society of Pennsylvania

The Quaker values of religious liberty, respect for others, and pacifism complemented practices that were already in place in the Delaware Valley. Penn's initial approach to the native peoples surpassed those of other colonial governors in that he wrote a letter of introduction to them in 1681 that was kind and respectful in tone and promised fair dealing. The letter was a calculated attempt to win the friendship of people who were losing their homes and lands they had enjoyed for generations to a large-scale land speculator.[iii] When William Penn and his thousands of fellow passengers arrived, they immediately outnumbered the established Europeans, and they pushed the Lenape from the prime land along the river at Philadelphia. For the Lenape, the change meant a loss of connection with the lower regions of the river, the loss of the strategic Schuylkill tributary, and the loss of large areas of cleared land. It meant the loss of the places where their ancestors were buried, the places where important medicinal plants grew, and the sacred places that were key to the culture and religion of the people. The Lenape withdrew to the north and west, but they met periodically with William Penn and his lieutenants as adept politicians. Penn himself reported, "He indeed deserves the name of Wise who outwits [the Lenape] in any treaty concerning a matter they understand." [iv] The Lenape could threaten violence while counting on the Quaker peace testimony to avert bloodshed. Despite a new wave of disease causing a sharp decline in their numbers, [9] the native peoples were able to maintain their sovereignty and independence through the merger and consolidation of communities, and by their skillful management of their relationship with the Quaker government.

The Lenape and William Penn appeared to have had a cordial and trusting relationship, but unfortunately, Penn spent only about 10% of the remainder of his life in the New World. His agents and sons, and even the Quaker settlers, did not always treat the indigenous peoples in accordance with the values that Penn did, and land

[9] the total population loss has been estimated as being up to a 95% decline by multiple sources

expropriation became a source of recurring conflict. The Lenape also felt threatened by the plantation system's dependence on slave labor, which included Indian slaves imported from Southern states. The Lenape were alarmed that the practice would lead to their own enslavement, and they insisted that the Pennsylvania government act. In 1706, the Pennsylvania Assembly passed a law to prevent the importation of enslaved Indians, because their purchase "from Carolina or other places hath been observed to give the Indians of this province some umbrage for suspicion and dissatisfaction." [v]

In summary, eastern Pennsylvania was once densely populated by the Lenape, and despite rapidly declining numbers after the arrival of Europeans, they remained firmly in control of the region of the Delaware Valley until Penn's arrival. Their way of life, which embraced personal freedom, multiculturalism, and religious tolerance, was well established before the Quakers landed. These values became their imprint on the region's culture, contributing to the foundations of democracy and the beginnings of the abolition of slavery. Many of their names for streams and villages are still in use, and many of their trails have become modern roads. Although most of the Lenape eventually died or were displaced from the area, some did remain on their ancestral lands, "hiding in plain sight" after adopting European customs. Their descendants continue to contribute to life in the Delaware Valley today.

PIONEER DAYS IN BUCKS COUNTY

In 1681, William Penn began to sell shares of Pennsylvania land to investors in order to pay off his debts and to cover the costs of colonizing. By the time he set sail in October of 1682, he had sold over 300,000 acres, and within four years, he had sold over 700,000 acres of Pennsylvania land to about 600 investors, making possible the rapid development of the new colony. [vi]

A detail of Thomas Holme's 1687 map of Pennsylvania, showing Bucks County

The land along the west bank of the Delaware River was purchased promptly from the Lenape and land grants were quickly distributed to the settlers. Lower Bucks County east of the Neshaminy Creek was purchased before Penn's arrival in 1682. Due to the continuing influx of colonists, the need for land was so great that the area west of the Neshaminy was already fairly well settled by the time it was purchased from the Lenape one year later. The northern boundary for these two parcels was set near the present-day village of Wrightstown because Penn could not pay the Lenape's asking price for central and northern Bucks County. The area to the north was important to the indigenous peoples since it was where Lenape survivors were merging to create new socially cohesive communities, and it also provided access to the Delaware River and to native lands in New Jersey. The Lenape prevented travel on the Delaware River above the Falls (near present-day Morrisville), and they threatened violence in order to protect that last stronghold. In 1686, when Israel Taylor surveyed this area, the sachems threatened to kill him. Deputy Governor Markham agreed to meet with the sachems, but the conflict was left unresolved. [10] Thomas Holme warned Penn that the sachem Tammany was threatening to burn the houses of settlers, and that "he hath so discouraged our people that we cannot get them to go to Bucks County to settle." [vii]

Notwithstanding the threats of violence and Holme's description of a discouraged people, expansion above Wrightstown began almost immediately. Perhaps the English settlers felt their safety was assured by a memorandum that had been attached to the Treaty of 1682, which stated "that if at any time an Englishman should by mistake seat himself upon land not purchased of the Indians, that the Indians shall not molest them before complaint made to the government where they shall receive satisfaction." [viii]

The early settlers came from a land of long-established culture and infrastructure only to be greeted by almost unimaginable hardship. Frontier Pennsylvania forests were dense with great trees, some of them hundreds of years old, and there was always a shortage of the manpower required to remove them. Not only did the land need to be

[10] The unsettled treaty later became the basis for the fraudulent Walking Purchase.

cleared for farming but wood was also needed for buildings, fences, furniture, barrels, and heating. Before the invention of the Franklin stove, twenty to thirty cords of wood were needed to heat a cabin for one season, requiring an entire month just to chop and split it. Some of the more fortunate settlers purchased land that had already been cleared and burned by the Lenape, and farm animals were available from the Swedes and Finns. [ix] Once the trees were felled, plowing commenced around the tree stumps, and family cows were tied to stakes or trees with vines. The earliest homes were log cabins, typically about twelve feet square; but if winter arrived before a barn could be built, the livestock were brought into the cabin during the coldest weeks to prevent them from freezing. [x]

An early log cabin built by Quakers in Falls Township

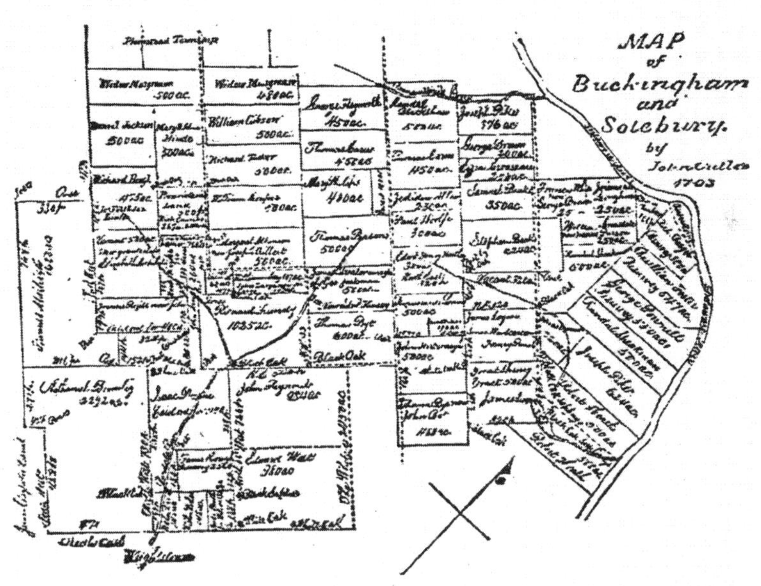

EARLY SETTLEMENT IN BUCKINGHAM AND PLUMSTEAD TOWNSHIPS

For most of its history, Plumstead Friends Meeting has been either part of, or supported by, Buckingham Friends Meeting. And so the history of Plumstead Meeting actually begins with Buckingham Township and Buckingham Meeting.

Above the northern boundary of lands purchased by Penn, Thomas Bye built a log cabin in 1699 in the vicinity of present day Lahaska. He was soon joined by about a dozen families who had migrated north from Falls Township. A surviving Buckingham Township survey from 1703 shows that nearly the entire township had been parceled out (though not necessarily occupied), and one reference mentions that six Indian villages were present in the township at that time.[xi]

In 1701, the "new settlers above Wrightstown" requested permission to meet among themselves on Sundays instead of making the eighteen-mile trip to Falls Meeting. This group would have been called "indulged" or "particular" out of Falls, that is, they were members of Falls Preparative Meeting who met elsewhere. Attendance at the Falls Meetinghouse would still have been required for the monthly Meeting for Business. In 1705, Falls Meeting agreed to build a log meetinghouse in Buckingham along the Lenni Lenape trail that connected Philadelphia to New Hope.

In 1720, Buckingham Meeting, "having for a long time with some hardships traveled a great way" to maintain their connection to Falls Meeting, had increased sufficiently in number to ask to become an independent meeting.[xii] By this time Buckingham Township had been created and its government organized.

Plumstead Township, adjacent to Buckingham's northern border, was named for first purchaser Francis Plumstead, an "iron monger" of London who never came to the New World. Thomas Brown was one of the earliest settlers, and after purchasing one thousand acres in the southwest corner of Plumstead Township around 1717, he located himself in the woods near present-day Dyerstown.[xiii] The first to encroach upon the solitude of Brown was John Dyer, also a Quaker. Dyer purchased 151 acres of land from Cephas Child in 1718, as well as improvements from Thomas Brown,[11] who subsequently moved further back into the woods near where the Plumstead Meetinghouse stands today. Dyer harnessed Pine Run to power the first grist mill in the township in 1722, [xiv]which then became an early trade center.

[11] MacReynolds, in Place Names in Bucks County says Dyer purchased 300 acres of land from Brown, and Battle, in History of Bucks County, states that Dyer purchased portions of the Arthur Cooke survey

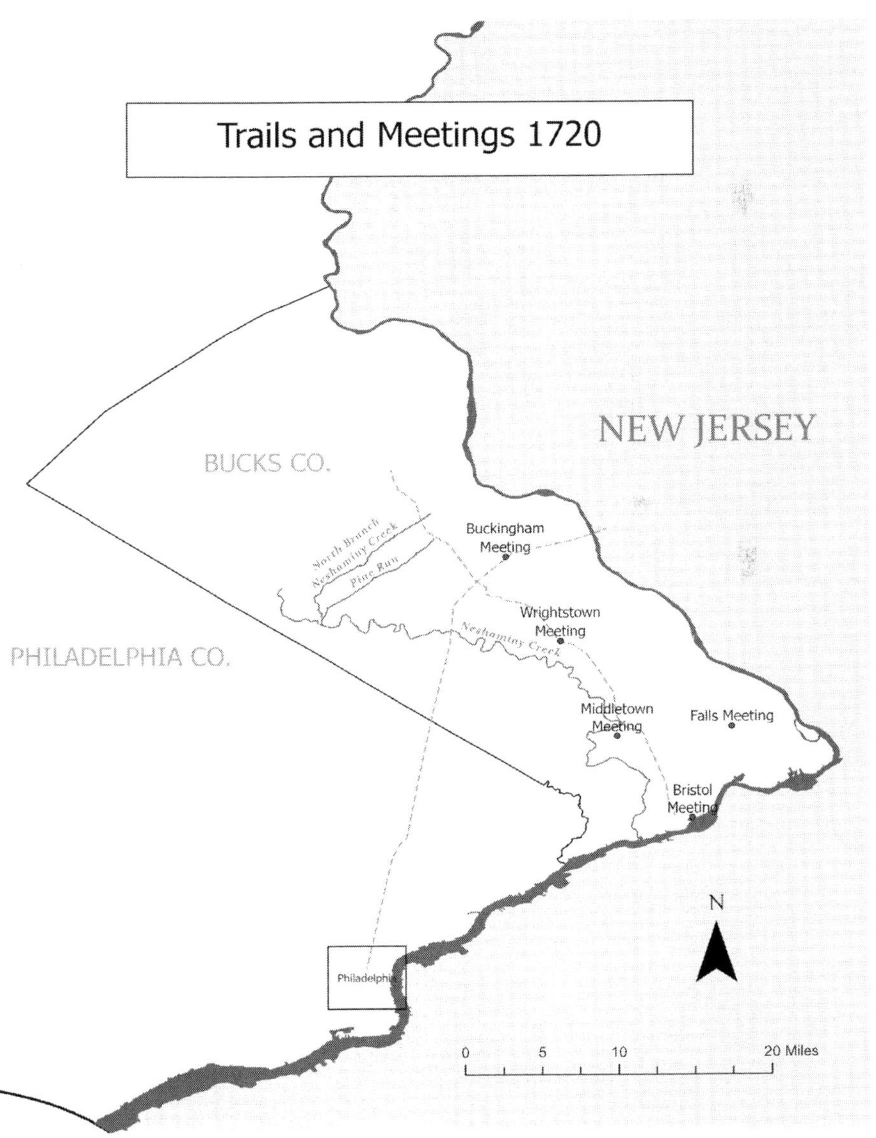

A map of the Quaker meetinghouses in Bucks County c. 1720, the Lenni Lenape trail, and the trail to the Lehigh Valley. Created by Whitley Gray

It is recorded that when John Dyer came into the township, wild animals were plenty, Indians numerous, and beavers built their dams across Pine Run. The Black Bear was common as far south as the valley of the same creek.[xv] Settlers found a wilderness of heavily timbered and rolling land, but there was also much poor land, and some was hardly worth cultivating. The eastern edge of the township was composed of rugged, rocky cliffs descending to the Delaware River.

The Lenape remained longer in Plumstead Township than in most other parts of the county. Tradition told of a native village of nine lodges in the northwest corner of the township whose residents remained there long after the township was settled by Europeans. They went to the Neshaminy Creek to catch fish, then abandoned that stream, paying frequent visits to the houses of settlers on baking day, where they were regaled with pies, cakes, etc., to conciliate their good-will.[xvi] Another early account from Buckingham Township reports that "Native simplicity reigned in its greatest extent. The difference between the families of the white man and the Indians, in many respects, was not great- when to live was the utmost hope, and to enjoy a bare sufficiency the greatest luxury." [xvii] In addition to the Lenape villages, there were many well established native trails, most notably the previously mentioned trail going northeast from Philadelphia, which later became York Road, and a trail going northwest from the Bristol area, which became Durham Road. [xviii]

A law passed in 1683 required inhabitants of the colony to work on the construction of roads and bridges or pay a fee.[xlx] In 1723 the Easton Road, probably the first in Plumstead Township, was extended from the Montgomery County line (and Willow Grove) to Dyer's mill. About the same time, Durham Road was opened southward from Brown's land (now Gardenville), following the Indian trail, where it met up with the section already opened to the Delaware River at Bristol.

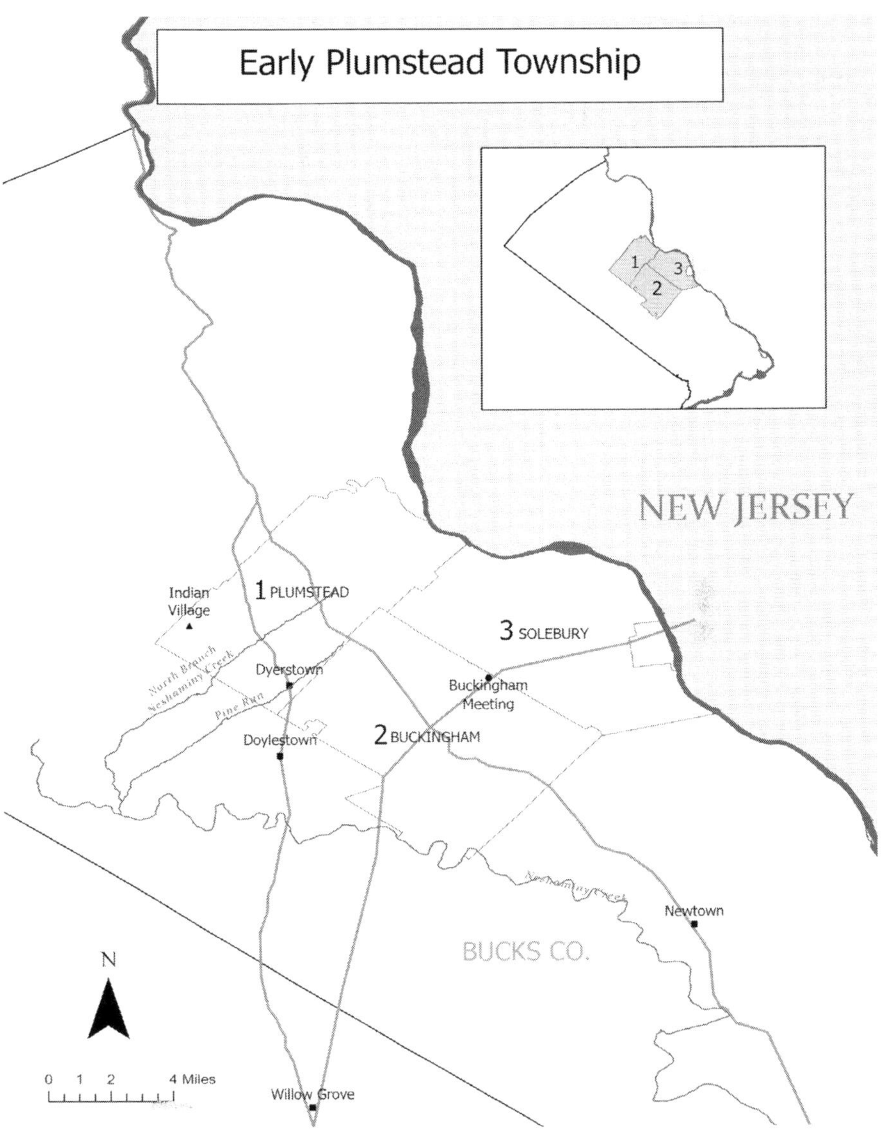

A map showing the location of (1) Plumstead, (2) Buckingham and (3) Solebury Townships. Details within Plumstead Township include Dyerstown along Pine Run Creek, and an Indian village. Three major roads are indicated, including two created from the Indian trails in the previous map, and a new road connecting Dyers mill to Willow Grove. These are present-day York Road (Route 263), Durham Road (Route 413), and Old Easton Road (Route 611). Created by Whitley Gray

These roads and others gave inhabitants ready access to the settled parts of Plumstead, adjoining townships, and markets in Philadelphia. [xx] But it must be remembered that they hardly allowed for anything beyond single file trains of pack horses.

English Quakers continued to push northward beyond Buckingham Township, but soon they were competing with Scots-Irish Presbyterians and German Mennonites for land. In 1710, German immigration to Pennsylvania increased significantly, and in 1727 alone, 50,000 Germans "overran" the wilderness of Lancaster, Montgomery, Berks and Bucks Counties. Plumstead Township was at the extreme northernmost limit of the comprehensive English Quaker settlement in Bucks County, which in turn, impacted Plumstead Meeting's membership. While Buckingham Meeting, only a little more than five miles to the south, outgrew three meetinghouses and divided itself into two additional Meetings, Plumstead would contract and eventually close for a number of decades.

VIGNETTE:

CEPHAS CHILD (1690-1756) XXI

Henry Child, father of Cephas, lived in Herford, England, and was granted five hundred acres in Plumstead Township by William Penn in 1681. Henry emigrated from England to Anne Arundel County, Maryland; Cephas was the only one of Henry's children to cross the Atlantic. In 1715, Henry conveyed to Cephas all of his undeveloped land in Plumstead, which was located in the westernmost part of the township. After the legal proceedings, Cephas, then twenty-five, walked more than 150 miles from below present day Baltimore to his new home in Bucks County, Pennsylvania.

Cephas married Mary Atkinson of Bucks County in 1716. Two years later, Cephas sold 151 acres of his holdings to John Dyer, who then established the first grist mill in Plumstead. Tragedy struck in 1723, when a fire destroyed the Childs' home and killed all of their four children. Cephas and Mary went on to have five additional sons, four of whom survived them.

The following letter was sent to Cephas from his father in 1738:

Ye 22^{d} of 3 mo., 1738.

Dear Child: — I thought I might have had a line from thee by some at our yearly meeting. I should be glad to hear what family thou hast, and how things prosper with thee. I desire thou mayest seek the Lord above all, that His wisdom may guide thee in all thy undertakings, that His name and truth may be honored by thee, that His blessings and mercies may be with thee, through the greatest mercy of the Lord . I and my family are in health, and thy sisters and their families. I gave thee account of thy brother's departure in my last letter to thee; so with love to thee and thy wife and friends, in the truth of our Lord Jesus Christ, I rest thy loving father,

Henry Child

In the Quaker community, Cephas was a weighty Friend, having served as clerk of Plumstead Particular Meeting, and keeper of the documentation for the Declaration of Trust of the property. As an Elder, Cephas was called on to handle delicate situations involving misconduct, and he encouraged the errant to do what was necessary to regain their good standing in the community. Cephas Child was also a member of the Provincial Assembly from 1747 to 1748, at a time when Quakers dominated politics in the colony.

Cephas Child died in 1756, contributing as an Elder until the end of his life. The meeting minutes record: "Our esteemed Friend Cephas Child, who many years served this Meeting in the Place of an Elder for Plumstead Particular Meeting being deceased, and Plumstead Friends having nominated for that service Thomas Vickers and Daniel Stradling, the Meeting approves and confirms the choice till further appointment." [xxii]

Surely Cephas lived up to the meaning of his name: "the rock."

CHAPTER TWO:

THE ESTABLISHMENT OF PLUMSTEAD MEETING

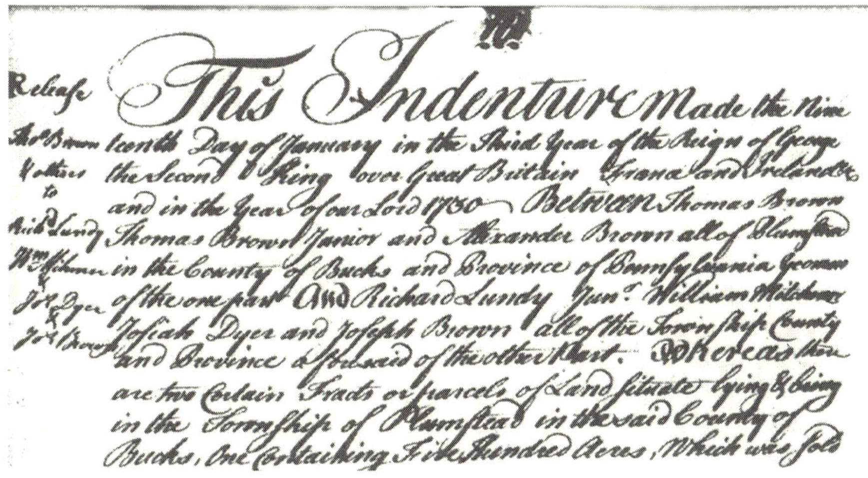

Release Thos Brown & others to Rich. Lundy Wm Mitchener Jos. Dyer & Jos. Brown

This Indenture Made the Nineteenth Day of January in the Third Year of the Reign of George the Second King over Great Britain France and Ireland &c. and in the Year of our Lord 1730 Between Thomas Brown Thomas Brown Junior and Alexander Brown all of Plumstead in the County of Bucks and Province of Pennsylvania Yeoman of the one part And Richard Lundy Jun.r William Mitchener Josiah Dyer and Joseph Brown all of the Township County and Province aforesaid of the other Part. Whereas there are two Certain Tracts or parcels of Land situate lying & being in the Township of Plumstead in the said County of Bucks, One Containing Five Hundred Acres, Which was Sold

The thousand acres in Plumstead that Thomas Brown and his wife had purchased were on a sloping hillside crossed at the bottom by Pine Run. Their holdings continued south, across the township line, to include an additional five hundred acres in the northwest corner of Buckingham Township. Thomas and Mary were the parents of nine children, the youngest born in 1709.

Although we do not have the specifics of the Brown family life, most Quaker farmers planted wheat as their primary crop, which was more lucrative than raising livestock and not prone to the fluctuations of the tobacco market. Although well supplied with land, first-generation Quaker households tended to live rustically. A typical farm had forty to fifty acres cultivated, a half dozen horses and cows, and some pigs and sheep. The family had a bed, a table, and three chairs, but no cupboards, and so they stored their goods in wooden boxes and trunks. They ate on pewter plates with spoons and their hands; most did not own any knives or forks.[xxiii] The line between those who could thrive and those who could not was thin indeed and was perpetually threatened by a failed crop, illness, alcoholism, and accidents. Luxuries of any kind, except spirituous liquors, were rarely thought of, or introduced, either of apparel, household furniture, or living. Necessity obliged the first settlers and their successors to wear a strong and coarse kind of dress; durable buckskin was used for breeches and sometimes for jackets. Flax and hemp fiber were used for shirts, and coarse fiber was used for trousers. Farm carts were owned by the best farmers. A very few had wagons before 1745, and carts for going to market were crudely made and easily overturned; the wild team sometimes ran away, and the gears often broke.[xxiv]

The township was quickly settled and improved. On an old draft of Plumstead Township, dated 1724, are marked about a dozen landowners, all near the Buckingham line.[xxv] By 1730, most of the original tracts were settled.[xxvi] The first notation of a Meeting for Worship in Plumstead was made in 1727, ten years after Thomas Brown's arrival in the area. Buckingham minutes record: "Att[sic] this Meeting John Dyer made application in behalf of himself and friends of Plumstead to have a Meeting every other first day during the winter for which request is left to further Consideration." This request was granted the following month.[xxvii] It has been noted that these early Plumstead

Friends met at the house of Thomas Brown[xxviii] as an indulged meeting out of Buckingham. The following year, permission was once again granted to have Plumstead Friends meet "amongst themselves" every other Sunday from November through March.

In May, 1730, the Buckingham minutes record: "At this Meeting Plumstead friends Requested that they might make application to the Quarterly Meeting for a settled Meeting amongst themselves with this Meetings free Consent, which the Meeting allows that they may make Application to the Quarterly upon that Account." [xxix]

At this Meeting those friends that were appoynted towards
the service of the Quarterly Meeting report upon the Account
of Plumsted friends having a Meeting Amongst them before
which the Quarterly Meeting Consented to, with Advice that
Plumsted friends take the Advice of the Monthly Meeting of
Place for building a Meeting house upon & graveyard allso,
And the Meeting Appoynts Thomas Watson Thomas Canby
Abraham Chapman Cephas Child John Dyer & Richard Lundy
junior for that service & that Plumsted friends keep the
Meeting at the house they built for a Scool house untill fur
=ther Order or appointment, their weeke day meeting to be
upon the fifth day of the weeke and this Meeting Appoynts
Richard Lundy junior & Thomas Browne junior to be Over
=seers untill further appointment.

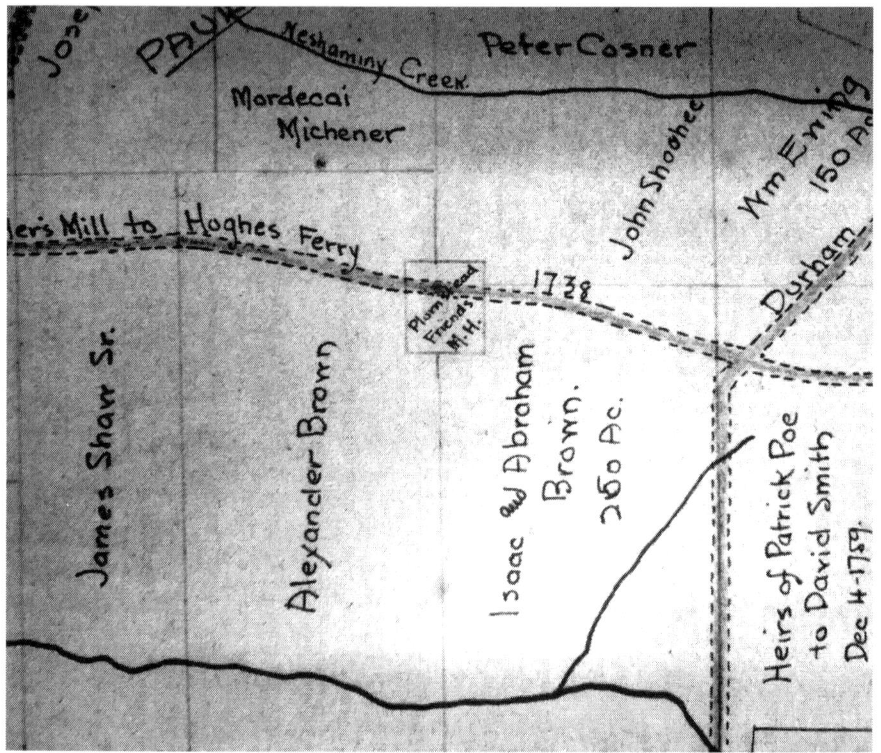

A recreated map showing the parcels of land in the area of Plumstead Friends Meeting for the year 1759, courtesy of the Bucks County Historical Society

That application was approved the following month, with the suggestion that Plumstead hold its Meeting for Worship temporarily in the Brown family schoolhouse, most likely a log cabin.[xxx] Thomas Brown senior's children were now in their twenties and thirties, and he had seen at least a dozen grandchildren born between 1720 and 1730. Building a schoolhouse was, no doubt, a priority for this family, and they had located it where their land was probably not suitable for cultivation, about a half a mile behind their home on a ridge running parallel to Pine Run. Plumstead Friends, after having met for several years on the property of Thomas Brown, were now offered part of his land for their permanent home. The minutes record in November of that year, that "According to a former minute the 2nd day of the 4th month Last, those friends that were appoynted [sic] to see the Ground and place to build a meetinghouse upon for Plumstead friends viz: Thomas Watson, Thomas Canby, Abraham Chapman, Cephas Child, John Dyer & Richard Lundy junior all met and viewed the place & ground & all of them thought the place near the schoolhouse & graveyard suitable." [xxxi] The location on the ridge was at the intersection of the holdings of Thomas Brown and two of his sons. Thomas Brown, Thomas Brown, Jr., and Alexander Brown together conveyed fifteen acres of their land in January, 1731, [12] to a group who would become the trustees of the meetinghouse property. Each of the Browns contributed five acres to the parcel, and each was paid five shillings. The grantees were Richard Lundy, junior, William Mitchener, Josiah Dyer and Joseph Brown. Minutes for the following month show that the deed for the land "is lodged in the hands of Joseph Brown and the declaration of trust in the hands of John Dyer." [xxxii]

The meetinghouse, also most likely a log building, [xxxiii]was constructed at the west side of the current burial ground.[13] It is always assumed that early log meetinghouses were gabled, since existing log meetinghouses are gabled.[xxxiv]

---

12 Recital of deed recorded in Book F, vol.3, p.114. It is dated January, 1730, which is the eleventh month of 1730 in the old style, but it would be the first month of 1731 in the modern calendar.

13 Journal of John Dyer: Entry for April 24, 1778 states that "Nathan Preston was buried where the old meetinghouse stood." Preston's plot is located at E-3.

An example of an early log Quaker meetinghouse, built in 1789 at Catawissa, Columbia County, PA

Plumstead Meeting was under the oversight of Buckingham, and attenders of Plumstead Friends Meeting remained members of Buckingham Preparative Meeting. Early on, overseers and elders for Plumstead were assigned by Buckingham from the Plumstead community so that problems could begin to be resolved before they were brought to the Buckingham Monthly Meeting. The fledgling community of Plumstead Friends Meeting was prospering. A separate clerk for Plumstead was first mentioned when Cephas Child was appointed in 1740. By 1749, the members of Plumstead Particular Meeting felt ready to build a stone meetinghouse.

The friends Belonging to Plumstead Informed this Meeting of their Intentions of Building a New Meetinghouse and aplyed to Buckingham friends for their Assistance both in Advice and Raising Money and Buckingham friends aproving thereof apoints John Scarbrough David Kinsey William Preston And Saml Wilson to Conferr With them and Compute as near as they Can the amount of the Charg and Make Report Next Meeting Concluded

Funds were raised through subscriptions (pledges) from the members of both Plumstead and Buckingham Meetings. David Kinsey was the carpenter, and his name, written with chalk, was long retained upon a hand rail in the interior.[xxxv] The new meetinghouse was located higher up the slope and behind the old one, and the Buckingham Monthly Meeting minutes of January 1754 indicated that the meetinghouse was completed. [xxxvi] Although specific details about the appearance of this meetinghouse have not survived, a typical meetinghouse of the settlement period in Philadelphia Yearly Meeting was a three-bay, one-cell building. The roof was most likely made of white oak shakes. The most reliable description came from a Friend who visited the Plumstead Meetinghouse about 1840 and described it as being two stories high. [xxxvii] Another source confirms this and adds that a smaller building, one story high and constructed of the same native stone, was attached to the end of the meetinghouse during the initial construction, for use as a school. [xxxviii]

The author's conception of the appearance of the first Plumstead meetinghouse based on written descriptions and the appearance of other meetinghouses of the same period.

The typical Quaker meetinghouse faced south,[14] and the facing benches for the ministers and elders were located along the north wall. Each seat in the minister's gallery was assigned to a specific person.[xxxix] Men and women in the congregation were seated separately during the worship service, with the men on the east benches, and the women on the west ones. A porch, containing a second entrance door, was often located at the west end of the exterior, allowing the

[14] Plumstead Meetinghouse faces southwest, perhaps to be parallel to Point Pleasant Pike, which had already been laid out by the time the stone meetinghouse was constructed.

women to alight from their carriages and gather on the porch while their husbands drove the carriage to the carriage shed. There was also typically a second-story gallery along the south wall for youth. Five years later, in 1759, Plumstead became an independent, preparative meeting, with its own membership and business meetings. [15] The men would have met for business in the east end, and the women in the west end. They would have been separated by a moveable wooden partition, probably located just west of the main entry door. (Remnants of this partition remain, since it was later recycled into a wainscoting in the current meetinghouse.) In 1761 Plumstead proposed to make an addition to the meetinghouse, which was approved by Buckingham Monthly Meeting, [xl] but there was no further mention in the minutes whether this plan was ever realized.

CHANGE COMES TO PLUMSTEAD TOWNSHIP

Relations with the Lenape had deteriorated; the English view of them had changed from being neighbors and trading partners to one of obstructing the settlement and the financial success of the colony. When iron ore was discovered in Durham in 1727, agent James Logan sent surveyors to the area, only to have them expelled by Lenape. When heavy immigration increased the demand for land, some German immigrants had settled in places without the permission of either the Lenape or the Proprietors of Pennsylvania. Pennsylvania officials believed that they needed to extend their authority and provide the institutions of government in these new settlements. But to do that, they first needed to obtain from the Indians a clear title to the land in the upper Delaware and Lehigh River valleys. The outcome was the

15 The Buckingham minutes of March 6, 1759 are the first to refer to the Plumstead Preparative Meeting. Plumstead, Solebury, and Buckingham Preparative Meetings were under the umbrella of Buckingham Monthly Meeting.

infamous 1737 Walking Purchase land swindle (see vignette). Its route, headed north on Durham Road from Wrightstown, passed within a half mile of the Plumstead Meetinghouse. It resulted in a permanent alienation between the English and the Lenape, who were then looking for a chance for revenge. During the French and Indian War, the Lenape killed over fifty settlers within Walking Purchase lands, including the Marshall family in nearby Tinicum Township.

The German Lutherans and Mennonites, as well as Scots-Irish Presbyterians, were also settling in Plumstead Township. Farmers with Irish surnames like Greer and Hart, and German farmers named Fretz, Gross, and Wismer lived near the meetinghouse. How were Friends, living among them and having no formal creed or clerical authority, to keep their identity? The answer was in adhering to Friends values, particularly in the home. Elders visited homes twice a year to be sure families were clear about the testimonies and to offer advice about childrearing. Marrying within the faith became particularly important, and, as the decades went by, breaching that line meant ever more dire consequences, including expulsion from the Society of Friends.

At this Meeting The Overseer of Plumstead Entred a Complaint Against Andrew Love for having taken too Mutch Strong drink Severall times and other Scandalous Actions when in drink to the great Reproach of our Profession & he appearing & brought a Paper of Condemnation to Acknowledge his Outgoings which + Proved not Satisfactory, which was Returned to him for a further Amendment as his Life & Conversation shall Demonstrate the Sincerity of an Amendment. Concluded

To be a united, distinctive community seemed particularly important as Quakers became a minority both in population and in politics around the middle of the century.[16]

In 1755, as war loomed ahead, Philadelphia Yearly Meeting issued a revised set of questions (The Queries) representing the important testimonies regarding behavior. The questions were to be answered in writing by each Monthly Meeting four times a year; this focus and accountability to the Yearly Meeting constituted a powerful and inclusive check on un-Quakerly forms of conduct. The Discipline, as a moral code, took more definite shape over time, and the means of enforcing it increased.[xli]

THE FRENCH AND INDIAN WAR

Reformers were uneasy about the ambiguities of Quakers holding governmental offices and participating in worldly affairs. Although now vastly outnumbered in the population as a whole, Quakers had a weighty voice in the Provincial Assembly. In accordance with the Friends peace testimony, there was no militia, nor were there any forts in Penn's colony. This absence of a military establishment left Pennsylvania defenseless while, in 1753, the French were building a line of forts from present day Erie to Pittsburgh. The war officially began in May 1754, and became more acute after Braddock's defeat in June 1755. Thomas Penn pressed for the disqualification of the Quaker Assemblymen, who were risking the loss of his charter by refusing to cooperate in prosecuting the war. Quaker reformers were pressing for the resignation of the Assemblymen as well, uncomfortable about Friends in government who had shown a

---

[16] Buckingham minutes are full of references to infractions such as "marrying out of unity," being "irregular and reproachful in conversation," "taking undue liberty with getting his money," "scandalous actions when in drink," "spectator at a horse race," and "printing and publishing a book without the advice and consent of Friends."

compromising spirit regarding pacifism. To complicate matters, many of the Assemblymen were also prominent leaders in Philadelphia Yearly Meeting, and they were expected to hold fast to Quaker values. A turning point came in 1756, when five legislators, including two Quakers, signed a recommendation to offer a bounty for Lenape scalps. [xlii] Thomas Penn declared war and offered the bounty, after which ten Quaker assemblymen resigned.

The French and Indian War was an inevitable conflict between the great European powers for control of the resources of North America. Its outcome was by no means certain. Ninety percent of the colony's former Europeans lived between the Appalachian Mountains and Philadelphia, and the remaining 10 percent on the frontier were especially vulnerable to attack. In 1756, Yearly Meeting recommended a collection to support suffering Friends on the frontier, and Friends were "exhorted to have a particular Regard in maintaining every Branch of our Discipline." [xliii] Friends were not to support the military even indirectly, and in 1758, the minutes reported "Friends should lovingly endeavor to convince such that have err'd in contributing towards furnishing wagons, etc. for conveying military stores [and] to visit all such as have been guilty of anything of that sort and labour with them." [xliv] A member of Plumstead Preparative Meeting was disowned for joining the fighting forces.

Decisions made during this period would prove to have lasting effects. Penn's "Holy Experiment" had ended with a declaration of war. When most of the Quakers resigned from the Provincial Assembly, it ended their political power and the Quaker majority within the government. Reformers within Philadelphia Yearly Meeting succeeded in the enforcement of disownments; from 1750 to 1790, Pennsylvania Quakers disowned almost 50 percent of the rising generation of Quaker young adults. [xlv] There had been definite benefits in the strengthening of Quaker values and identity, and taking the time for self-evaluation. But by limiting their growth and committing themselves to the sidelines of society, Quakers retired the notion that theirs could ever be a universalistic movement.

At this Meeting the Testimony against John Love was again considered, approv'd & sign'd by order of the Meeting. and the Meeting appoints John Thomas & Thomas Smith to deliver him a Copy of it & inform him of his Right of Appeal if he see Cause & report to next Meeting --- And it is ordered to be taken an Account of among the Minutes of this Meeting --- AND is as follows — viz

At our Monthly Meeting held at Buckingham the 2d of ye 4th Month 1759 WHEREAS Andrew Love late of Plumstead who being convinced of Friends Principles and made Profession of the Truth with us some Years, Before his Decease became concerned that his Children might be educated in the Principles of Friends And also appointed some Friends to take Care that his Children might be educated

cated and settled amongst Friends Notwithstanding his Son John Love hath so far Slighted his ~~deceased~~ Parents tender Concern ~~for him~~ as volantarily to inlist himself to be a Soldier contrary to the known Principles of Friends. the Consideration of which being for some Time under the Consideration of this Meeting and he not appearing nor offering any Satisfaction for his Misconduct we think it necessary for the clearing our Christian Profession to disown him the said John Love and do hereby declare we can have no further Unity with him as a Member of our Society until he become truly Sensible of his Outgoings & condemn the same to the Satisfaction of Friends which that he may do is our sincere desire

Signed in on Behalf & by Appointment of our said

Meeting by Paul Preston Clerk

VIGNETTE:

THE WALKING PURCHASE OF 1737

The Walking Purchase was land acquired by the sons of William Penn through a devastating betrayal of the Lenape. After Penn's death in 1718, management of Pennsylvania fell to his three sons and to his agent in the Land Office, James Logan. The sons were deeply in debt and sold vast tracts of land to settlers while ignoring Lenape claims. The Proprietors soon realized that optimal profitability depended on the Lenape relinquishing their rights, particularly to land in the Lehigh Valley. The indigenous peoples had become a nuisance, and ultimately were seen as expendable.

During negotiations that extended over several years, Logan told the Lenape that there was a document from 1686 in which the native peoples had promised to sell a tract of land, beginning at Wrightstown and extending north as far as a man could walk in a day and a half. This may have been an unsigned, unratified treaty or even an outright forgery. The Lenape were shown a distorted map and were told the route would go north when in fact it ran northwest. According to popular accounts, Lenape leaders assumed that about forty miles was the longest distance that could be covered under the existing conditions. Logan hired three extreme athletes, Edward Marshall, Solomon Jennings, and James Yeates to run (not walk) on a prepared trail. Boats were ready to assist them in crossing the streams. After the allotted eighteen hours, Marshall finished, reaching the vicinity of present-day Jim Thorpe, Pennsylvania, some sixty-six miles away. As a final insult, the northern boundary line was not drawn due east to the Delaware River, but was instead drawn at right angles to the route, resulting in an area of 1,200,000 acres, roughly equivalent to the size of Rhode Island, being transferred to the Penns.

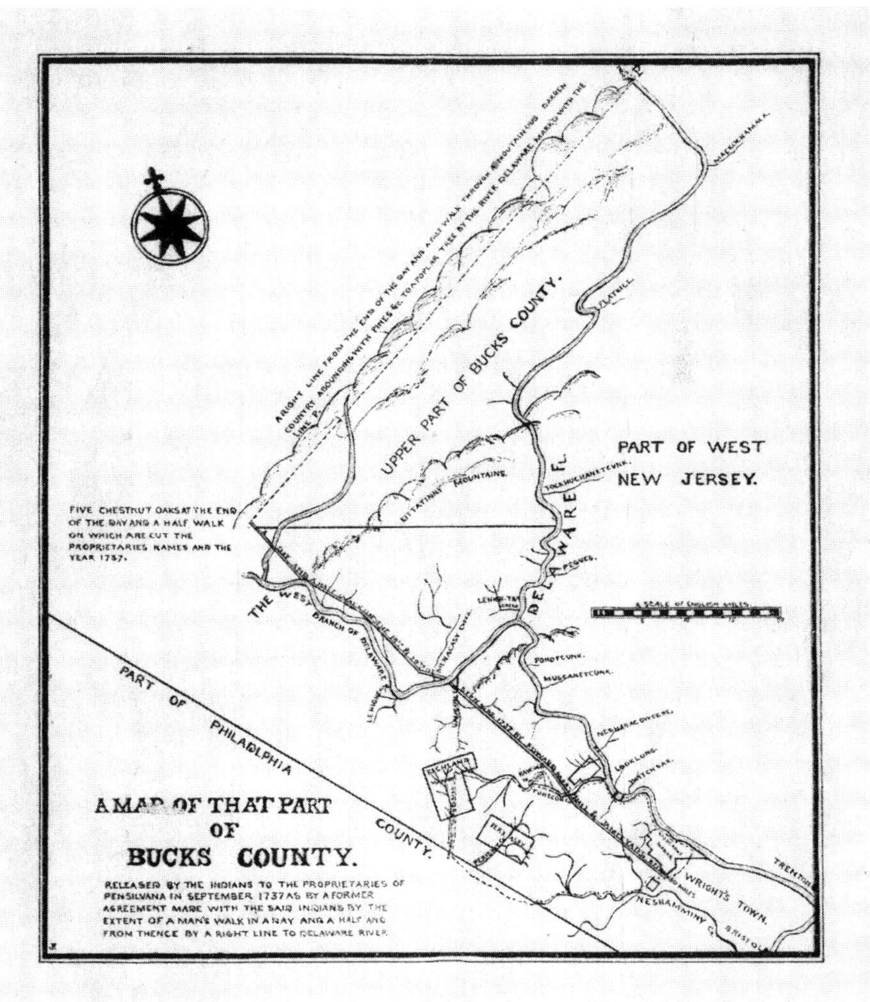

From the Collection of the Mercer Museum of the Bucks County Historical Society

Initially, the Lenape refused to surrender the territory, relenting only after Logan persuaded the Iroquois to act as his enforcers. Most of the Lenape left eastern Pennsylvania for the region of the Susquehanna River, but their resentment lingered. During the French and Indian War, they killed more than fifty settlers within Walking Purchase lands, including the family of Edward Marshall. In 2004, a lawsuit claiming 315 acres of this land was made by the Delaware Nation against the Commonwealth of Pennsylvania based on the claim that the land had been taken fraudulently from the owner in the Walking Purchase.

CHAPTER THREE:

REVOLUTION

This sign, commemorating Washington's Crossing the Delaware River, was painted by Quaker sign painter and Newtown resident Edward Hicks, a cousin of Elias Hicks. From the Collection of the Mercer Museum of the Bucks County Historical Society

Although the French and Indian War had resulted in France ceding all of its claims in North America to Britain, the war had been very costly. The Crown felt that because the colonies benefitted directly from the removal of foreign aggression, they were obligated to pay for some of the expense involved. The British intended to generate revenue from a tax that would, in addition, cover the cost of a standing army tasked to maintain peace between the Native Americans and the colonists. But settlers were accustomed to provincial governance and taxation within each colony, and resisted the imposition of a tax and a military presence from afar. An awareness of American self-reliance and loosening ties with Britain led to the beginning of a new political identity. Some families had been in North America for four generations and would never see the mother country.

The British began a series of taxations on printed material, then on imported goods, violating its own law that prohibited taxation without representation. Because the Board of Customs was headquartered in Boston, that area became an early focus of rebellion. But in some respects, life was continuing on as usual. Buckingham Meeting had outgrown its meetinghouse and was in the process of constructing a new one when, on April 13, 1768, the older building burned to the ground in the middle of the day.[xlvi] The first business meeting after that date was held in the Buckingham Meetinghouse stable, and thereafter was held in the Plumstead Meetinghouse until January 1769.[xlvii]

The journal of John Dyer (grandson of the early settler in Plumstead), recorded in 1771 such notable events as the killing of a very large bear and a local smallpox epidemic. The report from Plumstead Preparative Meeting to Buckingham for January 1772, however, revealed the larger issue of remaining pacifists during a time of rising tensions. Plumstead reported that the extracts from the minutes of the previous Yearly Meeting contained "Advice against defrauding the King of his Customs and dues and a recital of a Minute of the Year 1755 to that purpose," as well as advice "against taking or administering Oaths and against Friends soliciting for or accepting of offices or Stations in civil government, that may subject them to the temptations of violating our Christian Testimony, or electing or promoting other Friends to such stations." [xlviii]

John Dyer noted on July 20, 1775, that "this Day was appointed by the Congress (now sitting at Philadelphia) as a Day of publick[sic] Thanksgiving and prayer: George Washington is appointed Commander in Chief of the Continental Army and -------- there has been a battle fought at Boston some time ago." In the winter of 1775–1776, Friends from Pennsylvania, New Jersey, and elsewhere donated money and goods to relieve the sufferings of the inhabitants of Boston while the British occupied the city. [xlix] In those early days, Plumstead Quaker Thomas Dyer, an ardent pacifist, went so far as to forcibly take people's guns from them. The Friends community felt he was going too far, and they labored with him for a year. [l]

More common, however, was the opposite problem of dealing with Quakers who supported the military. Bucks Quarterly Meeting minutes noted in December 1776 "the Instability and Deviations of Many in Profession with us in These Times of commotion." [li]

Plumsted Preparative report contains, that Amos Shaw hath been out as a Soldier in the Army, therefore Jonathan Shaw, and John Carlile are appointed to treat with him on the Occasion and report to next Meeting.

Andrew Ellicott has paid a fine for not training therefore Thomas Watson and John Gillingham are appointed to treat with him on the occasion and report to next Meeting.

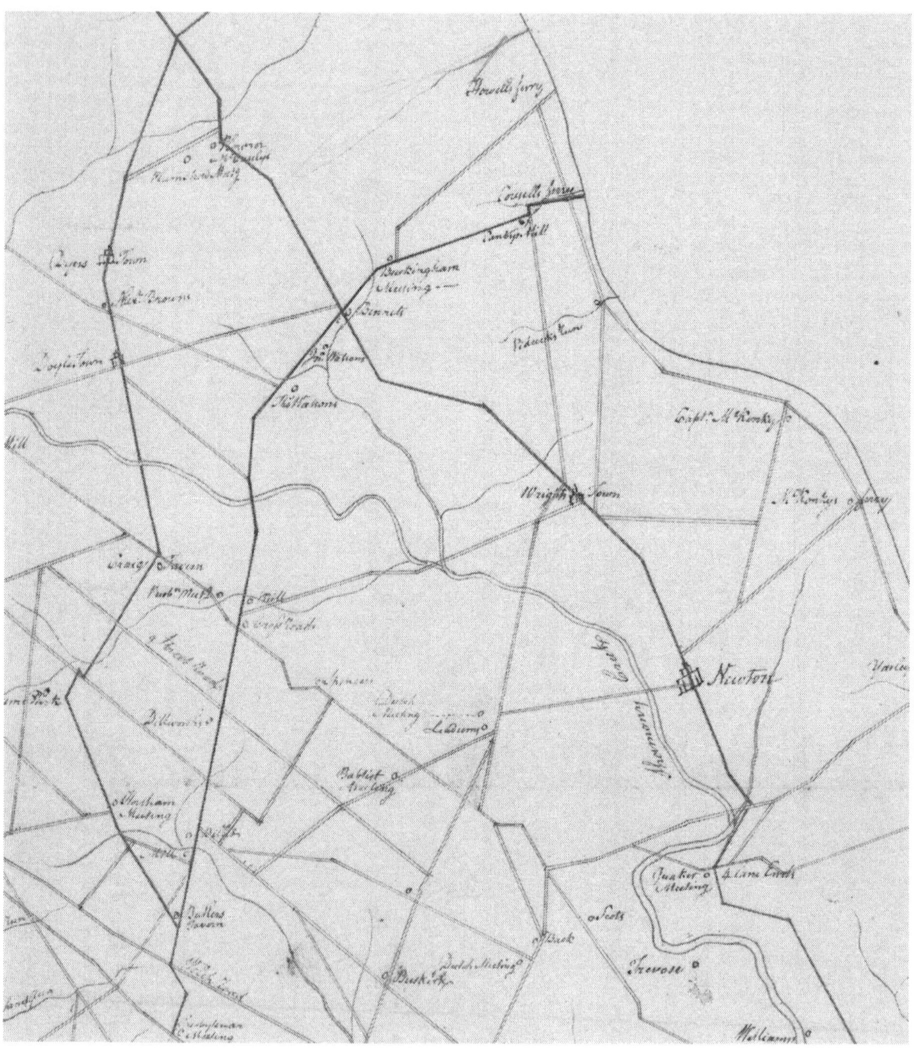

Detail from British General Henry Clinton's spy map c. 1777 showing the Plumstead Meetinghouse as a landmark. York Road, Easton Road and Durham Road have been darkened by the author to aid comparison to the maps in Chapter One. University of Michigan Library Digital Collections. William L. Clements Library Image Bank. Accessed: November 10, 2021.

The Plumstead reports to Buckingham are full of such concerns such as "[he] hath been out as a soldier in the Army," "[he] has paid a fine for not training," and "[he] is in the practice of training and making instruments for War."

That same month, the movement of Continental troops both before and after the Battle of Trenton remained about fifteen miles south of Plumstead in the vicinity of Newtown, Pennsylvania, leaving a minimal impact upon northern Bucks County. The greatest action would be seen the following year.

As the year 1777 unfolded, there was anticipation that the British would attack Philadelphia, the seat of the revolutionary government in the colonies. In August, Washington's army of about ten thousand men moved from New Jersey into Pennsylvania on the only road that connected New York to Philadelphia—the York Road that passed in front of the Buckingham Meetinghouse. The army camped for nearly two weeks about ten miles south of the meetinghouse at present day Hartsville. John Dyer remarked in his journal, "I saw the American army encamped near or at the Cross Roads, consisting of about 18,000 men in Bucks County." [lii] One cannot help but imagine the impact that a crowd of that size would have had upon the residents along York Road, a crowd bringing vermin and diseases, a crowd needing latrines, provisions of all sorts, and hay for their horses.[17] The troops would eventually engage British General Howe's forces at the Battle of the Brandywine. Washington's defeat resulted in the British occupation of Philadelphia on September 26, 1777, after which Howe garrisoned most of his troops in nearby Germantown. Washington's troops boldly (and unsuccessfully) attacked the British in Germantown on October 4, with a dense fog contributing to confusion and heavy casualties.

---

[17] By August 20, the tenth day at camp, sanitary conditions were becoming a problem and forage was becoming scarce (McNealy, p. 126).

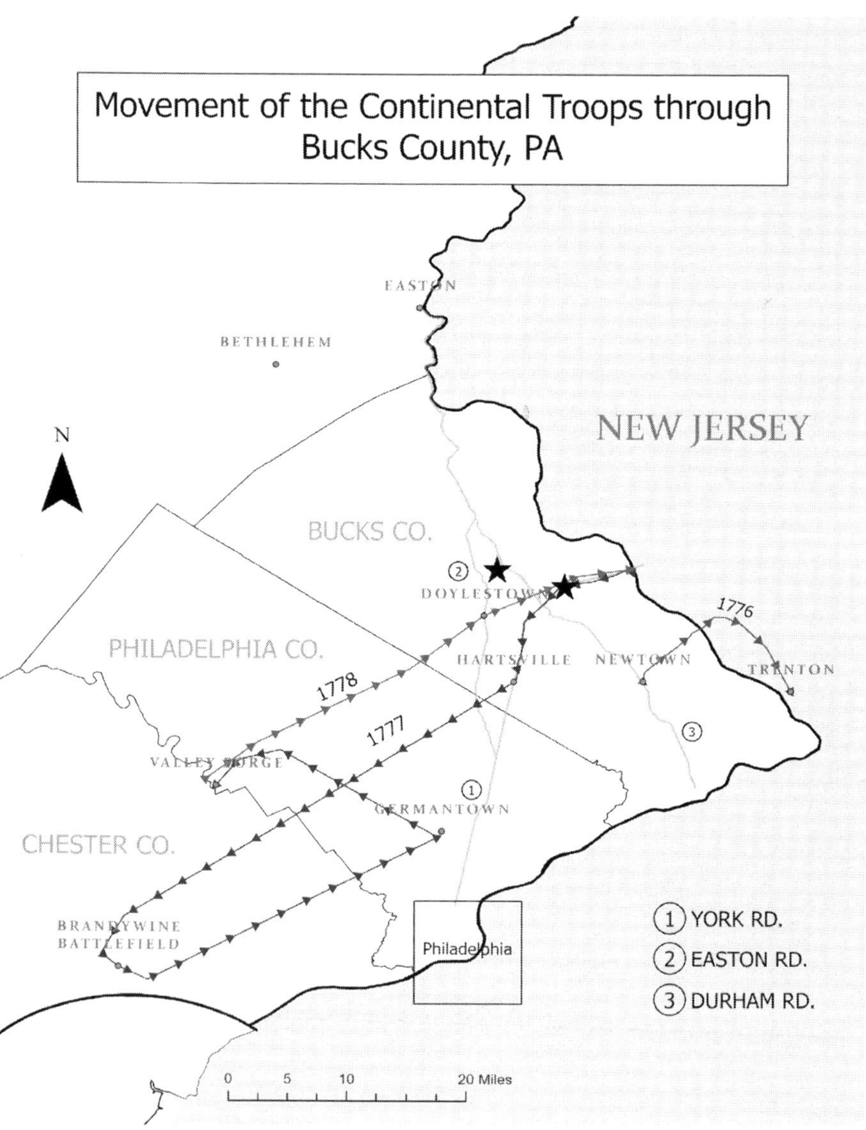

The movement of Continental Army troops through Bucks County in 1776,1777, and 1778. The stars indicate the locations of Buckingham and Plumstead Meetinghouses. Created by Whitley Gray

Treating the sick, plus five hundred or so wounded American soldiers, became a major problem. In 1776, Dr. William Shippen had been given directions by Congress and George Washington to set up a series of hospitals in Pennsylvania in order to get the anticipated casualties away from where the British might capture them. One of these hospitals was in Philadelphia, which now was unavailable. The other was in Bethlehem, which was full to overflowing and turning away the wounded.

The most seriously wounded were generally kept at field hospitals near where a battle had occurred. But the field hospitals, too, were now overrun, and area churches then became valued resources because their pews could be used as hospital beds. There were times when Quaker meetinghouses were forcibly possessed by the Continental Army. Uwchlan Monthly Meeting minutes noted, "The key of the meeting-house was demanded by some of the physicians of the Continental Army … The Friend who had care of the house refusing to deliver it, forcible entry was made into the house and stable." [liii] A November 1777 hospital report indicated that 259 soldiers were being cared for in Buckingham Township (239 of these were sick, 10 were convalescing, and 10 were wounded). [liv]

Location	Sick	Wounded	Convalesced	Total
		New Jersey		
Burlington	80	10	11	101
Trenton	112	0	102	214
Princeton	139	130	10	279
		Pennsylvania		
Buckingham	239	10	10	259
North Wales	100	0	59	159
Skippack	50	0	50	100
Easton	253	40	107	400
Bethlehem	161	80	142	383
Allentown	81	9	100	190
Reading				290
Lancaster				300
Manheim	17	5	40	62
		Maryland		
Baltimore				37

From "Easton's Missing Dead" in Journal of the American Revolution

In fall 1777, Dr. Francis Allison sent a number of the wounded of the Continental Army to the Plumstead Meetinghouse. A count of the sick and wounded totaled forty individuals: two died, ten discharged, and twenty-eight remaining. From there the survivors were moved to Lititz,[lv] which like Bethlehem, was a Moravian stronghold. Bloodstains stayed on the floor of the Plumstead Meetinghouse until the floor was replaced years later.[lvi]

When spring arrived in 1778, the people of Bucks County discovered how difficult life could be between two occupying armies. There were a half dozen or so skirmishes in the County, but perhaps more importantly, a policy had been put in place by the Patriots to block all trade between the countryside and the city. While the intention was to make life as difficult as possible for the British, it also deprived many Bucks County farmers of their livelihood of selling produce in the city. Moreover, it increased violence: Tory sympathizers in the County plundered provisions and smuggled them to the British in the city, and they burned a mill that had supplied blankets to the Patriots. By persisting in holding their meetings for worship at regularly scheduled places and times, and by crossing the belligerents' lines while doing the Society's business, Friends showed their religious mettle. [lvii]

Philadelphia Yearly Meeting had also been impacted by the 1778 blockade. The Committee for Sufferings decided to delegate some of its work to the various Quarters, asking in particular for them to help the Friends who had been imprisoned for refusing to sign the Oath of Allegiance and Abjuration. The work of PYM was additionally hindered by the arrest and exile to Virginia of twenty of its weightiest Friends, on suspicion of aiding the British.

Thirtieth Day of the Sixth Month 1778 Friends again assembled

The Committee named to take under their Consideration the Cases of the six Friends now in Lancaster Jail and the Circumstances Attending the same, produced a Report in Writing as Followeth to wit:

The Committee having considered the Cases of the six Friends now imprisoned in the common Jail at Lancaster, and being fully convinced that they are suffering for the Testimony of a Good Conscience, being by religious Considerations restrained from complying with the injunctions prescribed by some of the Laws Lately Enacted in Pennsylvania – We are United in believing that it is our Duty to lay their cases and the weight of their sufferings before those who have committed them to Prison, and should likewise apply to the Executive Council of Pennsylvania & endeavour to obtain their release, and we therefore propose that some Judicious Friends should be desired to apply to the Magistrates that committed them to Prison, and some others should attend the said Council and in such manner as they may be enabled in the wisdom of Truth, perform this service either in Person or Writing, as on Consideration they may Judge most expedient.

A portion of the advices from the 1778 Meeting for Sufferings regarding Quakers imprisoned for pacifism. The full text appears at the end of this chapter.

They were released eight months later but only after two of them had died.[lviii] Even worse, John Roberts of Merion and another Quaker would later be hanged.

Then, upon orders, the British broke camp from Philadelphia in June 1778, bound for New York. Washington's final foray through Bucks County was in pursuit of the British General Henry Clinton's troops as they marched from Philadelphia towards New York. Washington stayed overnight in Doylestown, after which the army marched north past the Buckingham Meetinghouse, crossed the Delaware River at New Hope, and headed to their victory at the Battle of Monmouth.

Though the armies had taken their action to other colonies, Pennsylvania Quakers remained under duress. Friends could have their property confiscated or be publicly whipped if they did not take the oath of allegiance. The *Journal of John Churchman*, [18] first published in 1778, was circulated as a way to inspire Quakers to maintain their discipline. Publication had to be suspended, however, due to the "scarcity of paper" and the "extraordinary cost of printing." [lix] In 1779 arrangements were made to have up to four thousand copies printed by subscription, and Plumstead Preparative Meeting ordered twenty-nine of these. [lx]

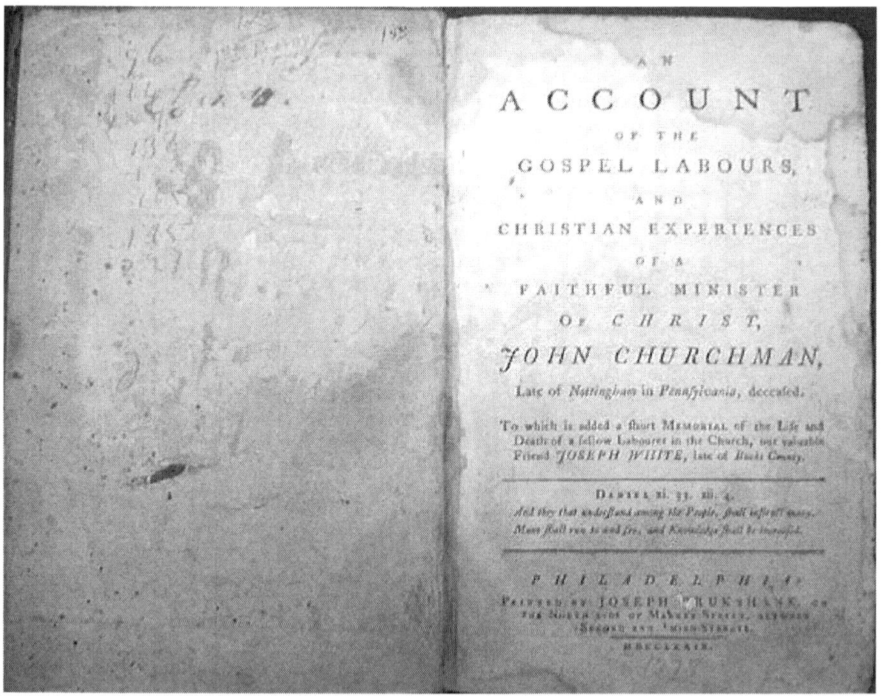

AN
ACCOUNT
OF THE
GOSPEL LABOURS,
AND
CHRISTIAN EXPERIENCES
OF A
FAITHFUL MINISTER
OF CHRIST,
JOHN CHURCHMAN,
Late of *Nottingham* in *Pennsylvania*, deceased.
To which is added a short Memorial of the Life and Death of a fellow Labourer in the Church, our valuable Friend *JOSEPH WHITE*, late of *Bucks County*.
Daniel xi. 33. xii. 4.
PHILADELPHIA:

[18] The Churchman family lived in Nottingham, Chester County. George Churchman made available the journal of his father, who had died in 1775, as a way to provide spiritual inspiration to Friends.

By withdrawing from politics and government during the Revolution, Quakers had earned the suspicion, distrust, and abuse of both the Patriots and the Loyalists. In the end, they did manage to maintain their pacifism fairly consistently while providing financial assistance to the deprived, healing the sick and injured, tending to the imprisoned, advocating for the abolition of slavery, and educating their children. To some Quakers, the financial losses suffered by wealthier Friends during the war was a welcome form of discipline. For others, their own wartime suffering and ostracism increased their sense of empathy, especially towards those kept as slaves, and propelled the issue of abolition beyond the Society. [lxi]

The American Revolution ended in 1783. By the time of the establishment of the new national government in 1789, an extended era of peace had already opened, and Friends had found an accepted place in their respective communities. Philadelphia Yearly Meeting took the occasion to present an address to President Washington, assuring him of their firm loyalty and pledging to contribute freely both to the necessary support of civil government and to the exigencies of the poor. Washington replied with a gracious statement of his high regard for the Quakers and the constructive role they played in society.[lxii]

THE DOAN GANG

While tensions were rising shortly before the Revolutionary War, Philadelphia Yearly Meeting issued a statement supporting payment of taxes to the Crown, and during the war, it had maintained contact with London Yearly Meeting. So despite the clear opposition of Friends to supporting any military activity, even indirectly, it is easy to see how Quakers might have been perceived as Tory sympathizers. The case of the notorious, outlaw Doan Gang of Plumstead, however, was of a completely different order of magnitude.

The Doan family came from England to New England in the 1630s, then migrated to Pennsylvania in 1696. The earlier generations became Quakers and settled just north of Dyer's mill. At the core of the Doan gang were five brothers—Moses, Aaron, Mahlon, Levi, and Joseph—and their cousin Abraham.

Because of the family's strong loyalist support during Revolutionary times, the local government had taxed them excessively and raided their crops. The brothers and their cousin retaliated in a reign of retribution led by Moses. They robbed tax collectors, became enemy spies, and stole hundreds of horses to aid the British. Moses, twenty-five, struck fear in the back country, dressed in long slicker jacket and wide-brimmed hat astride a coal-black mustang named Wild Devil. A master of disguise, he was British Army Gen. William Howe's "Eagle Spy," named for how precise his dispatches were. It was Moses who discovered unguarded Jamaica Pass, enabling Howe to swarm ten thousand Redcoats into Brooklyn to rout Washington's army at the Battle of Long Island on August 27, 1776. The decisive victory put the Continentals in flight to Philadelphia in what seemed the beginning of the end for the young rebellion. [lxiii]

Terry McNealy picks up the story: "The band included several others, friends and relatives not only from the Doans' home territory in Plumstead Township, but from other parts of southeastern Pennsylvania, New Jersey, and Maryland.

"...One of the first historically documented exploits of the Doan Gang was also their most spectacular feat. On the night of October 22, 1781, just three days after Cornwallis surrendered to Washington at Yorktown, a dozen or so of the gang rode into Newtown, forced their way into the home of county treasurer John Hart, took his keys and then stole the county treasury from the small office building near the courthouse.

Sketch of colonial Newtown showing (from left) the jail, the treasury building, and the courthouse. From www.buckslocalnews.com

"For several months, state and county officials fumed and investigated, but the identity of the robbers remained unknown. However, as the robberies continued a pattern quickly emerged. The victims were tax collectors, militia officers carrying payrolls, and other people who held government money. Some robberies were successful and others were bungled, but they effectively disrupted the functioning of local government and created turmoil for public officials.

"A break in the case came in the summer of 1782 when gang member Jesse Vickers was captured, tried, and sentenced to hang. In return for pardons, he and his brother Solomon, taken a few days after Jesse, confessed, naming gang members and giving details on many of the robberies.

"Using this information, the state Supreme Court began "procedures of outlawry" against all twenty-nine robbers and accomplices named by the Vickers. The procedure, rooted in medieval English law and never before used in Pennsylvania, required that an accused person be called to appear before three successive terms of court. Failing to appear, he would be declared literally outside the protection of the law. If subsequently captured, the penalty of the law, including execution, could be carried out without a trial.

"The gang continued its depredations, expanding its field of operations and sometimes striking several times in one night. The state retaliated, offering rewards and confiscating and selling the property of Joseph Doan, Sr.

"On February 10, 1783, tax collectors Daniel Hough, Joseph Dyer, and Jonathan Stout were all victims. On June 5, 1783, after robbing John Praul, a collector in Tinicum, and John Tucker of Buckingham, the perpetrators paid a visit to the tavern of Robert Gibson in Plumstead where they taunted the innkeeper and bragged of their exploits.

"Then on July 21, the gang committed six robberies, the last of which was at the inn of Colonel Robert Robinson, now the Dublin Inn. A posse took up the chase and captured Joseph, Jr., who had been shot in the jaw. After Joseph was packed off to jail in Philadelphia, the gang made threats to force his release- posting handwritten notices stating that if Joseph were not released they would commit murder and arson, and kidnap Frederick Muhlenberg, speaker of the state assembly.

"Just weeks later, on August 28, a chance remarks by a boy at a gristmill revealed that the Doans were hiding in a remote cabin near the Tohickon Creek. The miller raised the alarm and soon a posse surrounded the cabin. In the ensuing struggle, Moses Doan was shot dead and Captain William Kennedy of the militia mortally wounded. Levi and Abraham Doan escaped. The gang members who remained free soon scattered, seeking refuge far away from Bucks County.

"In 1784, Joseph Doan, Jr. pled guilty and was sentenced to death-for unknown reasons his outlawry was quashed by the state supreme court. But in September he escaped from the Newtown jail before his hanging could be carried out. He eventually made his way into Canada, where he raised a family and lived to a ripe old age.[19] At some point Mahlon was arrested and jailed, but he also escaped and fled to New York City.

"That summer, Aaron was captured and condemned under his outlawry, but appeals saved him- that and the struggle between the State's executive and judicial branches over powers and jurisdiction. He spent nearly three years in a miserable Philadelphia prison before being pardoned and ordered to leave the United States in May of 1787.

"In 1785 and 1786, there was a new rash of robberies of public officers in Bucks County, and the county treasury was robbed for a second time. Gang members were captured including Abraham and Levi Doan. Aaron Doan, who had not yet left the country as ordered, was arrested, charged with robbery and condemned to hang in New Jersey that summer. He was reprieved under the gallows at Newark, N.J., on July 29, 1788, largely through the efforts of his father, Joseph Doan, Sr., and this time prudently left for Canada.

"Joseph Sr. was not as successful with Abraham and Levi, who were still subject to outlawry. This time the state was in no mood for mercy. Abraham and Levi were hanged at Philadelphia on September 24, 1788, their bodies brought back to their old home in Plumstead and buried at the Friends meetinghouse there, just outside the cemetery wall.

---

19 Davis relates that, in the 1830s, Joseph Doan returned to Pennsylvania as an old man and said that he had escaped from the Newtown jail by unlocking the door with a key he had made, and he then scaled the yard wall (Davis, Lectures, p.309)

The grave of Levi Doan located outside the Plumstead burial ground wall. The original marker is made of native stone; this one was placed after 1935. Photo by Dafydd Jones

"The legacy of the Doans is mixed. They fought for a lost cause, carrying on the struggle for at least ten years. Were they motivated by loyalty to the Crown, or did they simply cloak their greed in expressions of Tory sentiment? They may have started out with strong political motives and high ideals from which desperate circumstances forced them to stray. ..Perhaps their best legacy is the vivid example of how history can be complex, ambiguous, and ironic." [lxiv]

As this book was going to print, new research being done by the Mercer Museum about the Doans was brought to the author's attention. There is some rather convincing evidence that Abraham and Levi Doan were buried across the street from the Plumstead Meetinghouse, and not close to the burial ground at all. The native stone outside the burial ground wall may mark another grave of that era, perhaps that of the Revolutionary War soldiers who died in the meetinghouse. The research is currently ongoing.

VIGNETTE:

SOME ADVICE TRANSMITTED FROM THE MEETING FOR SUFFERINGS

Some Advice transmitted from the Meeting for Sufferings was read in this Meeting being as followeth:

At a Meeting for Sufferings held in Philadelphia for Pennsylvania and New Jersey the 29th of the 6th month

The intercourse between this City and the Country having been interrupted, it became the Concern of several of the Quarterly Meetings to nominate committees to give the necessary attention to the Cases of those who were or might be brought under Sufferings for the Testimony of Truth- some Friends of those Committee Members of this Meeting from the Western and Chester Quarters acquainted the Meeting that the following Friends to wit John Hollingsworth, Thomas Buckman, Charles Dingee, James Smith, Stephen Howel, and Joshua Bennet have been for a Considerable time (some of them upwards of ten months) confined in the common Jail at Lancaster where they now remain, because they cannot for Conscience sake take the test or Affirmation of Allegiance and Abjuration or comply with the requisitions as directed and prescribed by the acts of Assembly passed in Pennsylvania. This Meeting feeling a sympathy with them in their present situation and being desirous that some further step may be taken to forward their release upon a right foundation as truth may open the way—and their Case involves that of the whole society, the entering into the circumstances alluding the same to be necessary, and in order that the meeting may be more fully informed, the following Friends, to wit Israel Pemberton, James Pemberton, James Thornton, Thomas Lightfoot, Samuel Allison, Nicholas Waln, Mark Miller, John Evans, John Parry, Isaac Jackson, and William Jackson are desired to prepare and digest what may be fit to be further opened in the meeting respecting this subject, and report to an adjournment tomorrow morning at the 10 Hour.

Thirtieth day of the Sixth Month 1778 Friends again assembled. The committee named to take under their consideration the Cases of the six Friends now in Lancaster Jail and the Circumstances- Attending the same, produced a Report in Writing as Followeth to wit:

The Committee having considered the Cases of the six Friends now imprisoned in the common Jail at Lancaster, and being fully convinced that they are suffering for the Testimony of a Good Conscience, being by religious Considerations restrained from complying with the injunction prescribed by some of the Laws lately enacted in Pennsylvania- We are United in believing that it is our Duty to lay their cases and the weight of their sufferings before those who have committed them to Prison, and should likewise apply to the Executive Council of Pennsylvania & endeavor to obtain their release, and we therefore propose that some Judicious Friends should be desired to apply to the Magistrates that committed them to Prison, and some others should attend the said Council and in such manner as they may be enabled in the wisdom of Truth, perform this service either in Person or in Writing, as on Consideration they may Judge most expedient.

And on Consideration as what is necessary to be proposed to Friends in general on the subject of the declaration of Allegiance and abjuration, required by some late Laws passed by the legislation that now preside in

Pennsylvania and New Jersey, having several times met and deliberated thereon, we have the satisfaction, find we are united in Judgement, That consistent with our religious Principals we cannot comply with the requisitions of those laws- As we cannot be instrumental in setting up or pulling down of any Government: but it becomes us to show forth a peaceable and meek behavior to all men, seeking their good and to live a useful, sober and religious life without joining ourselves with any party of War, or with the spirit of strife and Contention now prevailing and believe that if our Conduct is thus Uniform and our hopes fixed on the omnipotent arm for relief, that in time he will amply reward us with lasting peace, which has been the experience of our friends in times past, and we hope is of some who are now under Sufferings and in order to communicate this union of sentiment on so important a subject and preserve our brethren in religious profession from wounding their own minds and bringing burthen upon Themselves and others, we think it expedient to recommend to the Committee appointed by the several monthly meetings to assist in suffering cases in pursuance of the advice of our Yearly Meeting with other faithful Friends, speedily appoint a --- meeting, or meetings of conference with each other in the several quarters, In which the grounds of our principals on this Head may be opened and our objections against complying with those Laws fully explained and a united Concern maintained to strengthen each other in the way of Truth and Righteousness, and to warn and caution in the spirit of Love and meekness those who may be in danger of deviating.

Which report having been deliberately read over and also considered by Paragraphs is approved and recommended to the observation of Friends in Pennsylvania and New Jersey or elsewhere within the verge of this Yearly Meeting, where Laws of the like nature are or may be passed- And friends are directed as way may open to spread the concern and promote a uniformity of conduct in the members of our society in respect to the subject matter of report- And the Clerk is directed to send Coppys [sic] thereof to the monthly and quarterly meetings.

Coppyed [sic] from the minutes of our said Meeting for sufferings by Nicholas Waln, Clerk

Which is recommended to the deep consideration of our Members individually.

Thomas Watson, Aaron Phillips, Timothy Smith, Samuel Armitage, Thomas Fell junior, Edmond Smith, Hugh Ely, John Kinsey, Francis Good, and Benjamin Cutler are added to assist the Committee appointed the sixth day of the first Month 1777 to advise and assist in suffering cases as more fully expressed in the Minute- And they are directed to be vigilant in the exercise of their Trust.

Read at Buckingham Monthly Meeting 7th d /9th month/ 1778.

CHAPTER FOUR:

THE STATE OF THE CHURCH

1st of the 10mo & 5th of the Week. On renewed Attention to the State of the Church as set forth in the Summary of the Reports from the Quarters, a lively Sence of the prevailing influence of a Worldly Spirit, as the radical Cause of Defection

The opening remarks of the extracts of the 1795 Philadelphia Yearly Meeting minutes appear in full in the appendix

Philadelphia Yearly Meeting and its constituent quarterly and monthly meetings were headed for, in the words of Rufus Jones, "the greatest tragedy in Quaker history." The seeds of that tragedy were sown decades before, no doubt with the best of intentions, and resulted in a bitter conflict that would ultimately directly impact Plumstead Friends Meeting. That is the subject of this chapter.

The Society of Friends of the Truth at its founding emphasized the experience of inner spiritual guidance and power. Quakerism was a revival of the early Christian church, and followed Christ's teachings of love. The Biblical phrase "the kingdom of God is within" was, for

Quakers, a personal, deeply felt experience. The realization that a capacity to love, i.e., "that of God," existed in all people led to the Quaker testimonies of integrity, equality, tolerance, and pacifism. Religion was not something one learned about on Sundays; it was a way of life. However, by rejecting the authority, forms, and sacraments of the Church of England, Quakers became besieged and imprisoned by the English government. Quakerism endured and became consolidated in spite of—or because of—this persecution. It forced early Quakers to be consistent in demonstrating their values and behavior, or risk further punishment.

The establishment of Pennsylvania as a utopian society marked a manifestation of, and flowering, of Quaker culture. As the wilderness was cleared, Quakers created a government without a military, and a family characterized by loving respect, equality of the sexes, and supportive care. In addition to being a religious body, the Quaker meeting functioned as an extended family and was the center of the community. It provided a library and a school, a social safety net for the less fortunate, and discipline for the errant.

Quakers had developed a structure that allowed for the encouragement of spiritual thought and pastoral care without an ordained religious leader. During Meeting for Worship, anyone could speak their spiritual leadings, but some seemed more gifted in this area than others. A gifted person could ask to be named a minister, and with the meeting's approval, he or she would then sit facing the congregation on the elevated benches as a recognized leader for life. The objective of the minister was not to teach so much as to direct his hearers to their own Inward Teacher.[lxv] He (or she) might begin by quoting a portion of Scripture, then elaborate upon the sense of the passage or how it should be applied. [lxvi]In addition to the ministers on the facing bench were the Elders, noted for their quiet wisdom and good judgement, whose job was to deepen the spiritual life of the community as well as to advise and support the ministers. [lxvii] A third group of leaders, the overseers, were vigilant about the welfare of the congregation as a whole, and provided discipline, pastoral care, and financial assistance. Communication between meetings was fostered by traveling ministers, the exchange of letters, and by the appointment of representatives who attended regional gatherings every three months. Representatives from all meetings gathered yearly in Philadelphia. The Quarterly and Yearly Meetings were also organizations in themselves which contained committees that conducted business, and met more frequently.

A distinctly Quaker culture and moral code developed over the course of decades, and was printed in a Yearly Meeting publication called the Book of Discipline. It cautioned, for example, against "the corrupt conversation of the world" and the problem of strong drink. Early on, the Discipline admonished against marrying outside the Society, which Friends increasingly believed would weaken the proper observance of Quaker conduct in the home. The culture of the Quaker family and the nurturing of children in the faith was considered by Yearly Meeting as vital to the future strength of the Society.

By the middle of the eighteenth century, Pennsylvania's population and society had become predominantly non-Quaker. As war loomed with France, it was clear that the holy experiment of a utopian colony had slipped out of reach. No longer able to reshape the entire society, Friends focused on improving themselves, with a desire to return to the uniformity of early Friends as a matter of integrity. In 1755, the Yearly Meeting leaders provided a list of fourteenth questions (queries) in the Book of Discipline that focused on specific behaviors, which in turn, were a reflection of Quaker values. Chief among these were both a strong statement regarding the bearing of arms, and a firm directive for the immediate disownment of anyone marrying out of the

Society. Laxity in the enforcement of the latter rule came increasingly to be seen as allowing the infiltration of influences weakening strict adherence to Friends' principles. [lxviii] Infractions or any "disorder" were discussed openly in monthly business meetings, and a public apology from the transgressor was expected. Every three months, a written report, such as follows, was sent to Philadelphia. In addition, and in order to assure absolute compliance, Yearly Meeting appointed thirty ministers, elders and other leaders to visit and inspect the discipline of the monthly and quarterly meetings. It is important to note that the concern of the leadership was more for the identity, integrity, reputation, and values of the Society than it was for the spiritual state of any delinquent member.[lxix]

The Buckingham and Plumstead Preparative Meetings needed to have their answers to the queries approved by Buckingham Monthly Meeting, and so their answers were recorded in the minutes. An example [20] follows:

> *"The queries were read, and answers to them being brought up from our several preparative meetings the substance of them as collected and approved by this Meeting is as follows, viz:*
>
> 1. **Are all our religious meetings for worship and discipline duly attended, the hour observed, and are Friends preserved from sleeping, or any other unbecoming behavior therein?**
>
> *Our meetings are all attended, those on the first days of the week and for discipline by the greatest part of our members; those on other days of the week much neglected by many; the hour is nearly*

[20] This example is from 1st d./8th mo./1791, but the queries and responses went essentially unchanged for decades.

observed by most who attend; drowsiness and sleeping at times prevail over some of which some care is taken; other unbecoming behavior generally guarded against in Meeting.

2. Is Love and Unity maintained amongst you, as becomes the followers of Christ? Are tale-bearing, back biting and evil reports discouraged? And where any differences arise, are endeavors used to end them?

   Love and unity (we believe) in a good degree are maintained amongst us generally, though not by all of us, so fully as they ought to be, some are careful to discourage tale bearing, back biting, and spreading evil reports: But all are not so circumspect herein as they should be. When differences appear endeavors are used to end them.

3. Are Friends careful to bring us those under their direction, in plainness of speech, behavior, and apparel, in frequent reading the Holy Scriptures, to restrain them from reading pernicious Books, and the corrupt conversation of the world?

   Some of our members endeavor to bring up those under their direction agreeable to the contents of the third query: But in many, a more general care therein than prevails is manifestly needed.

4. Are Friends careful to discourage the unnecessary distillation, or use of spirituous liquors, frequenting of taverns or places of diversion, and to keep in true moderation and temperance on the account of births, marriages, burials and other occasions?

   Our members are (we believe) generally careful to discourage the unnecessary distillation and use of spirituous liquors: But some we fear have not been so circumspect herein as they ought to be. Moderation and temperance in a good degree prevail at births, marriages, burials, and other occasions.

5. Are poor Friends necessities duly inspected, they relieved or assisted in such business as they are capable of? Do their children freely partake of learning to fit them for business? And are they and other Friends children placed among Friends?

   The poor are taken care of. Friends' children (a few instances excepted) are placed among Friends.

6. Do you maintain a faithful testimony against oaths, an hireling ministry, bearing arms, training, or military services, being concerned in any fraudulent or clandestine trade, buying or vending goods so imported, or prize goods; and against encouraging lotteries of any kind?

   Excepting one instance of a member taking an oath, (which is under care) we know of none among us chargeable of a breach of any part of this query.

7. Are Friends clear of importing, purchasing, disposing of, or holding mankind as slaves? And do they use well those who are set free, and are necessarily under their care, and not in circumstances, through non-age or incapacity to minister to their own necessities? And are they careful to educate and encourage them in a religious and virtuous life?

   There are no slaves among us. And of those set free care is taken.

8. Are Friends careful to live within the bounds of their circumstances, and to avoid launching into trade or business beyond their ability to manage, as becomes our religious profession? Are they punctual to their promises, and just in the payment of their debts, and are such as give reasonable ground for fear on these accounts, timely labored with for their preservation or recovery?

Some of our members are not so careful to perform their promises in the payments of their debts as they ought to be. A general care appears to prevail among us, in respect to the other parts of the eighth query.

9. **Do you take care regularly to deal with all offenders, in the spirit of meekness and wisdom, without partiality or unnecessary delay, in order that where any continue obstinate, judgement according to the nature of the case may be placed upon them in the Authority of Truth?**

Offenders as their offences come to our knowledge (we believe) are dealt with in a good degree of meekness. Yet an increase of zeal for the right restoration of such would be profitable.

The effect of the discipline of 1755 was felt widely throughout Philadelphia Yearly Meeting, resulting in a strong reemphasis in exclusion of worldliness from the Quaker way of life, [lxx]and a prolonged period of self-examination and accountability. Theologically, there was an increased emphasis upon the direct contact with God by attending to the Inner Light, called Quietism. There had always been discipline from the overseers in earlier times, but now the moral code was more defined, and the discipline enforced more consistently. Oversight and enforcement by Yearly Meeting minimized the local Quaker decision making process of discerning the "sense of the meeting." This affront to the autonomy of the monthly meetings was initially resisted by some, and in Bucks Quarterly Meeting only one meeting had complied by February 1756. [lxxi]

Yearly Meeting meant business when it came to conformity. Bradford Monthly Meeting in Chester County proved to be the most obstinate opponent to reform. The committee appointed by the 1762

Yearly Meeting to inspect quarterly and monthly meetings learned that Bradford had refused to answer the standard queries about the behavior and business of Friends and their meetings. Bradford had answered them earlier, and honestly. But when Western Quarterly Meeting told Bradford Friends that it did not like the behavior reported in the answers, Bradford refused to continue answering. That refusal started the trouble, and triggered an inspection which disclosed that even more was amiss. In February 1763, the committee told Bradford that it appeared incapable of transacting "the affairs of the Truth," and that unless it removed the disorders, or applied without delay to the Quarterly Meeting for help, Bradford Monthly Meeting would be dissolved and its members distributed among the other monthly meetings. Consistent oversight and attendance by Quarterly and Yearly Meeting representatives over a period of years gradually improved the situation.[21]

This powerful check on un-Quakerly behavior resulted in increasing numbers of members being condemned, or disowned by the Society. It is difficult to determine how much of an impact these measures had on the absolute population of Quakers in the late eighteenth century, since there were new members added from convincements, and some disowned members were reinstated after a while. Children continued to enter from large Quaker families, but in ever decreasing amounts when newlyweds were disowned for marriage disorders. Nonetheless, it is evident that no later than 1820, Quakers were declining in absolute numbers as well as relative to the population as a whole.

21 Marietta, pp 78–79. Note that the Western Quarter was closer to the front lines of the French and Indian War. Marietta discusses the situation in more detail, and the payment of military taxes was a central issue.

Being clear about what was important to Friends and being unified about it did, however, produce a revitalization. Friends were better able to support one another in strict observance of the peace testimony, which was especially important during the Revolutionary War.

The fact that Quakers wished to create a distinct culture and identity that rejected avarice, militarism and dissipating distraction did not mean they wished to isolate themselves completely from others. Friends felt an urgent need to focus attention on the more oppressed segments of American society and supported one another as they engaged with the larger community about unpopular issues. In 1762, the encouragement of moves toward abolition of slave holding in Quaker households was emphasized. Five years later, the minutes for Buckingham noted "There was produced at this Meeting 23 small Books intitled [sic] *A Caution & Warning to great Britain & her colonies* which were divided in the usual Proportion." [lxxii] The full title went on: "in a short representation of the calamitous state of the enslaved Negroes in the British dominions," authored by Anthony Bezenet.

Buckingham formed a committee to labor with their slave owners, which noted the following year that "The Friends appointed to inspect in Relation to Negroes, reported that they have visited such as keep them— and think that some further Care in that respect may be of some use." [lxxiii] By 1774, the Yearly Meeting directed disownment for any Friend holding slaves or engaged in commerce in slaves. [lxxiv] In time, Friends would broadened their abolitionist campaign, with a unified voice, in the arena of national politics.

Work was also needed to aid the Indians. Yearly Meeting called for "benevolence and charitable exertions" towards the "distressed inhabitants of the wilderness, with grateful remembrance of the kindness of their predecessors to ours in the early settlement of this country."

A

CAUTION

TO

GREAT BRITAIN

AND

Her COLONIES,

IN

A short REPRESENTATION of
The CALAMITOUS STATE of the
ENSLAVED NEGROES
In the BRITISH DOMINIONS.

By ANT. BENEZET.

PHILADELPHIA Printed:
LONDON Reprinted, 1767.

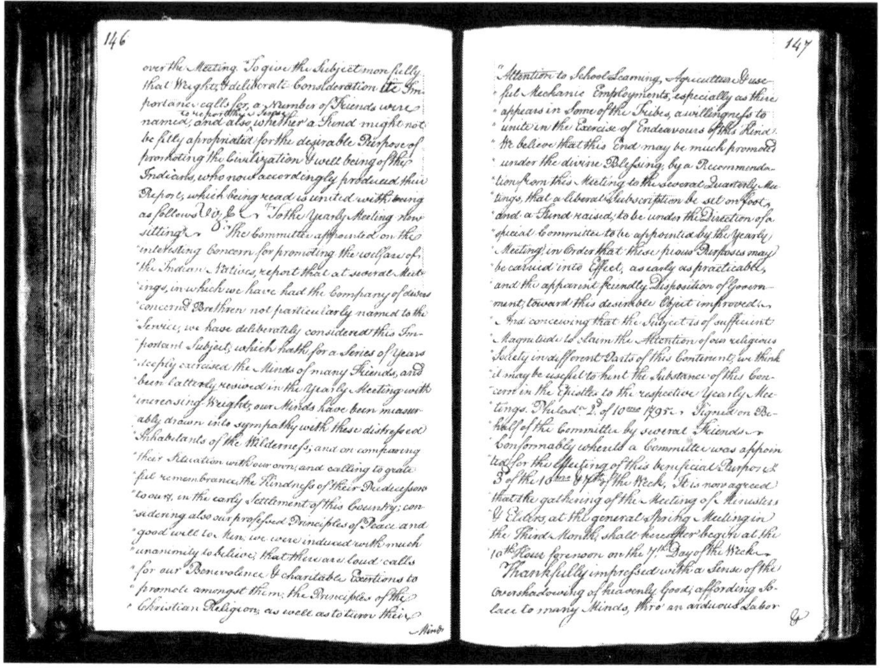

146

over the Meeting. To give the Subject more fully that Weight & deliberate Consideration its Importance calls for, a Number of Friends were named; and also whether a Fund might not (to report thereon) be fitly appropriated for the desirable Purpose of promoting the Civilization & well being of the Indians, who now accordingly produced their Report, which being read is united with being as follows Viz &c. "To the Yearly Meeting now sitting. The Committee appointed on the "interesting Concern for promoting the welfare of "the Indian Natives, report that at several Meet-"ings, in which we have had the Company of divers "concern'd Brethren not particularly named to the "Service; we have deliberately considered this Im-"portant Subject, which hath for a Series of Years "deeply exercised the Minds of many Friends, and "been latterly revived in the Yearly Meeting with "increasing Weight; our Minds have been measur-"ably drawn into sympathy with these distressed "Inhabitants of the Wilderness; and on comparing "their Situation with our own; and calling to grate-"ful remembrance the Kindness of their Predecessors "to ours, in the early Settlement of this Country; con-"sidering also our professed Principles of Peace and "good will to Men; we were induced with much "unanimity to believe; that there are loud calls "for our Benevolence & charitable Exertions to "promote amongst them; the Principles of the "Christian Religion; as well as to turn their Minds

147

"Attention to School Learning, Agriculture & use-"ful Mechanic Employments, especially as there "appears in Some of the Tribes, a willingness to "unite in the Exercise of Endeavours of this Kind. "We believe that this End may be much promoted "under the divine Blessing, by a Recommenda-"tion from this Meeting to the several Quarterly Mee-"tings, that a liberal Subscription be set on foot, "and a Fund raised, to be under the Direction of a "special Committee to be appointed by the Yearly "Meeting, in Order that these pious Purposes may "be carried into Effect, as early as practicable, "and the apparent friendly Disposition of Govern-"ment, toward this desirable Object improved. "And conceiving that the Subject is of sufficient "Magnitude to claim the Attention of our religious "Society in different Parts of this Continent, we think "it may be useful to hint the Substance of this Con-"cern in the Epistles to the respective Yearly Mee-"tings. Philad^a. 2^d. of 10mo 1795. Signed on Be-"half of the Committee by several Friends. Conformably whereto a Committee was appointed for the Effecting of this beneficial Purpose. 3 of the 10mo & 7th of the Week, It is now agreed that the gathering of the Meeting of Ministers & Elders, at the general Spring Meeting in the Third Month, shall hereafter begin at the 10th Hour forenoon on the 7th Day of the Week. Thankfully impressed with a Sense of the Overshadowing of heavenly Good; affording Solace to many Minds, thro' an arduous Labor &

Extracts of Philadelphia Yearly Meeting minutes as recorded in the Buckingham Monthly Meeting minutes 7th d/12th mo./1795

The following year, Plumstead raised a donation in excess of £25 for native peoples, which was paid to the treasurer of the Yearly Meeting Committee for Indian Affairs.

The establishment of Quaker schools was another priority, particularly as a way to provide a "guarded education" away from the potentially corrupting influences of non-Quaker society. Yearly Meeting reported in 1787: "Attention being given to the general accounts of Care exercised in most places for the Promotion of well-regulated schools for the Instruction of the Youth in useful Learning there appears a ground of hope that this momentous concern is gradually making Way in the minds of Friends, to be extended not only to the children of Friends of more easy circumstances in life but also to the offspring of those who are Poor and of the Black people whose condition give them a claim to that benefit consistent with a sense of this Meeting." [lxxv]By the end of the century there were approximately sixty Friends schools in Pennsylvania, including a boarding school at Westtown. Quakers were also careful to place their children who had apprenticeships with other Quaker families whenever possible.

America was now a new nation, and getting established as an experiment of democracy. Secularized versions of Quaker norms went on to become bedrock American Ideals. The Constitution of the United States, written in Philadelphia, owes much to Penn's democratic philosophy as manifested in his Frame of Government. The Frame incorporates the ideas that government exists by consent of the governed, that Church and State be separated, and that branches of government be separated as well. Implicit in this form of government was the notion that the common man could be trusted to make rational and responsible decisions. It was not the theocracy of New England, nor the aristocracy of the South, but the liberal democracy of the middle colonies that determined America's future.

Philadelphia Yearly Meeting was located in the temporary capital city of this nation. In 1793, a yellow fever epidemic swept through the city, killing about 10 percent of its inhabitants. The disease reappeared in 1797, and that year, Robert Kirkbride was named by Plumstead Meeting to attend Philadelphia Yearly Meeting sessions. Kirkbride contracted yellow fever, dying a few days after returning home, the disease also causing the death of his young daughter, Anna. [lxxvi]

In Philadelphia, a large, two-acre Quaker burying ground was located at Fourth and Arch Streets, surrounded by five-foot-high brick walls. In 1803, the walls were raised to a height of nine feet, supposedly as a reaction to having numerous dead yellow fever victims thrown over the walls into the graveyard. Philadelphia Yearly Meeting built its meetinghouse, the largest in the nation, behind those high walls the following year. The raising of the walls, was in some respects symbolic of the attitude of Yearly Meeting leadership, but events would soon prove they could not wall off changing times forever.[lxxvii]

CRISIS AND SEPARATION

Quaker Quietism rested in the belief that any involvement of the human will, reason, emotion, and intellect contaminated the experience of the Inner Light. In the eighteenth century, the emphasis upon God's direct contact with the believer had become so pronounced that all acceptable preaching was deemed to come from a "feeling" of God's presence. Ministers gave messages in a special sing-song chant that seemed to distinguish them from human utterances.[lxxviii] Those who accepted the divine promptings and preached as they were led were accorded extraordinary deference by the membership; however, the ministers' journals show the psychic cost of their dread of presuming to speak for God when self-will might become dominant at any instant.

In the early nineteenth century, Quakers in significant numbers on both sides of the Atlantic modified or repudiated Quietism. No longer seen as a perfect guarantor of truth, Quietism seemed inadequate to buttress the faith against the challenges of the enlightenment. The effrontery of a minister presuming to speak for God and then misquoting Scripture, prophesying inaccurately, using bad grammar, or showing the effects of indigestion made educated Quakers search for a more factual grounding for their faith. [lxxix]

An evangelical emphasis appeared among English and Irish Friends at the end of the eighteenth century. Evangelicalism maintained the belief that salvation is achieved through faith in Jesus' atonement, that there is an inner transformational conversion experience within those receiving salvation, that the Bible is inerrant and the ultimate authority, and that it is important to spread this message to others. A 1779 amendment to the English Act of Toleration, which substituted belief in the Scriptures for belief in Anglican Church doctrine as the discriminatory test, had broad social and economic consequences for dissenters, and provided a strong incentive for all denominations in Britain to emphasize the authority of the Bible.

The first Quakers on both sides of the Atlantic who became evangelicals tended to be well educated, prosperous, and activists for reforms, such as in asylums and penitentiaries. In their reading of Quaker history, they claimed to have discovered that the founders were evangelicals. Hence in their ministry and writings they sought to return Quakerism to its roots. They preserved the silent meeting and plain style of life but stressed the outward work of Jesus' crucifixion and resurrection as the means to salvation. [lxxx]

The rapid increase in immigration, the loss of political power and prestige, and the static quality of traditional Quaker worship stimulated prominent Philadelphia Friends to rethink the implications of their faith. Evangelical Friends (later called "Orthodox") tended to live in the city, own stock, participate in commercial enterprises, and favor close cooperation with other religious groups. They belonged to Bible societies and supported a variety of reform groups. Compared to their country counterparts, Philadelphia Quakers were more likely to have visited England or entertained English Friends in their homes. Since they stood very much in awe of English respectability, the advocacy of evangelical doctrines by English ministers and the fear of condemnation by English Friends were powerful influences.

In opposition to the evangelicals were those Friends whom opponents later termed "Hicksites," but who, like the Orthodox, thought of themselves simply as Friends. The largest faction among Hicksites were traditional Quietists who accepted the truth of the Scripture, the divinity of Christ, and the resurrection, but the symbol they emphasized above all else was the indwelling Christ. The authenticity of a minister's remarks was demonstrated by the manner of his or her life rather than by reliance on Scripture. Brinton relates that these ministers "could remind their hearers of unpleasant truths in such a spirit of love and genuineness that no anger resulted. Their faces shone with the peace of God because inner strains had been removed by obedience to divine will." [lxxxi]

Within the Hicksite membership was a distinct minority who also wanted to revitalize Friends, but their objection to the evangelical's literal reading of the Bible was based upon a newly emerging view of church history. In this view, concepts such as the Trinity were interpreted in light of the times in which they were formulated. A second influence was the rational philosophical movement, which sought a clear, reasonable and benevolent concept of God which would appeal to the intellect. [lxxxii]Benjamin Ferris (later the Hicksite leader in Delaware) praised "the spirit of free inquiry" in a debate of forty-two letters published throughout the years 1821–22 against the Presbyterian minister Eliphalet Gilbert. The clash between Ferris's group and the Philadelphia Quaker elders was the opening salvo of the conflict that became linked with Hick's name. [lxxxiii]

Seeing the dangers from these movements, the evangelicals sought to root out heresy among Quakers by promoting education and Bible reading. Traveling ministers propagated evangelical Quakerism along the eastern seaboard of America, and sought to impose their definition of Quakerism on the Quietist Friends who opposed theological learning (which was thought to reduce the reliance on direct experience of God). The evangelicals, who were noted for their cooperation with other Protestants in a wide variety of causes, seemed suspicious to Quietists. All the symbols most precious to the evangelicals seemed a reason for distrust. Friends, the Quietists insisted, should resist becoming like Presbyterians.[lxxxiv]

Evangelicalism flourished best when there was an enemy to identify, and the immediate danger came from Elias Hicks, a traveling minister from Long Island. As early as 1808, an English Quaker traveling with Hicks found his communications unsound, but many American Friends found Hicks an inspiring preacher. He would argue the most critical spiritual issues by powerful reasoning in accordance with everyday common sense. [lxxxv]

Engraving by Peter Maverick 1830

During his travels throughout America Hicks attracted large crowds and kept the full support of his monthly, quarterly, and yearly meetings in New York.[lxxxvi] He also carried on the most voluminous correspondence of any Quaker minister. Hicks has been described as an extreme Quietist. He believed that the Bible must be interpreted by the Spirit, not by human effort, learning, or Bible societies. He made the historical life, death, and resurrection of Jesus into symbols of timeless truth that must be understood directly through the Light within each person. Although Hicks never rejected the divinity of Christ or the inspiration of the Bible, his attitude toward biblical history made human dependence upon atonement by Christ's death unessential.[lxxxvii] The elders feared Hicks was advocating Deism, even though he specifically attacked Deism. In addition, Hicks' opposition to the wealth and power of Friends in cities such as Philadelphia led some of the leading Quakers to fear his intent was to undermine their power and authority. [lxxxviii]

The evangelicals (later called Orthodox) experienced frustration in dealing with what seemed a fundamental challenge to the faith. Elias Hicks, who had spent his entire adult life in the service of Friends, appeared maddeningly evasive when the normally reliable disciplinary procedures failed to work. When elders and ministers attempted to declare the fundamentals of Christianity, they encountered opposition from country Friends both in the Meeting for Sufferings and the Yearly Meeting. Worse, they found themselves pilloried as pseudo-Presbyterians and aristocrats who were opposing the inward light, holy living, and the autonomy of local meetings. In an age when rural-urban tensions were high and elitism was decried as un-American, these devout Philadelphia Quakers whose prosperity was a blessing from God and a tribute to their hard work were being defied by less educated, less affluent, less sophisticated farmers. Unable to silence Hicks or even gain an acknowledgment of error from him, and hampered by his sympathizers even within the city, the Orthodox decided to employ the agencies at their disposal: the support of English Friends, predominance in the Meeting for Sufferings, and Ministers and Elders, and the clerkship of the Yearly Meeting.[lxxxix]

Prominent English evangelical Quakers Elizabeth Robson, William Forster, and Anna Braithwaite traveled multiple times to the United States to denounce Hicks's views. The embargo and the War of 1812 had cut off most contact from 1808 to 1816, and the kindest of the English public Friends had been replaced by harsher ones. They all denounced Hicks's doctrines in his presence, in large groups, and in private homes, and at times tried in vain to keep him from speaking.[xc] Braithwaite twice met Hicks in his home for prolonged theological discussions, after which she published an unflattering tract refuting his views. Subsequent printed debate followed.

Both parties seemed easily offended, and exalting in the indignity of being insulted and having his/her integrity questioned. The inability of these well-known Friends to respect and understand one another only increased the tension and polarization between the factions at large. Regretfully, when Anna Braithwaite returned to America in 1827, she was rebuffed and objected to by many. In 1841, long after the death of Elias Hicks, she admitted, "Calm reflection and observation of passing events, and of persons, have convinced me that I took an exaggerated view of the state of society with reference to Hicksism." [xci]

As a Public Friend, Hicks had traveled widely, and he had been to Philadelphia multiple times over a period of decades. In 1822, Hicks visited Green Street Meeting families, and received a request for a private meeting with elders representing all the Philadelphia Meetings. Hicks' position was that he was not accountable to them, but he finally consented, out of courtesy, as long as witnesses could be present. The elders then refused to meet, saying Hicks's conditions were not private, and stated as Hicks was "unwilling hear and disprove the charges brought against thee, we feel it a duty to declare that we cannot have religious unity with thy conduct nor with the doctrines thou art charged with promulgating." [xcii] In a follow up letter, they concluded, "As thou hast on thy part closed the door against the brotherly care and endeavours of the elders here for thy benefit, and for the clearing our religious profession, this matter appears of such serious magnitude, so interesting to the peace, harmony, and well-being of society, that we think it ought to claim the weighty attention of thy Friends at home." [xciii]

Just a few days later, in January 1823, the Meeting for Sufferings Issued a lengthy statement of doctrine, a kind of Quaker Creed, signed by the clerk of PYM. [22] This declaration of faith was not approved

[22] This statement of doctrine appears in full in the appendix.

by Yearly Meeting, and so was ineffective to stop Elias Hicks. During the next two years, elders made multiple, persistent efforts to discredit and silence Elias Hicks. When Hicks next returned to Philadelphia, he drew even larger crowds of those who were curious to see who the fuss was all about.[xciv]

What started as a controversy over one person then spread to the issue of governance. Those who were most devout, most attuned to communicating the will of God, in short, the ministers and elders, had a predominant role in arriving at decisions within Yearly Meeting. Supposedly all Friends had the right to attend and to speak at Quarterly and Yearly Meetings, but in practice the clerk recognized only representatives, minsters, and elders. If Friends had confidence in the impartiality of the clerk, then the Yearly Meeting could operate successfully. However, the central institutions of Philadelphia Yearly Meeting, that is, the Meeting for Sufferings (which functioned as a kind of executive committee) and the Select Meeting of Ministers and Elders, were also the main centers of strength of the Orthodox believers. During the late 1820s, a majority of Friends became convinced that the clerk had become a spokesperson for the evangelical faction. [xcv]

Hicks visited Green Street Meeting in Philadelphia in 1826 and was welcomed by its members, but several elders attempted to forbid him from preaching. What followed was a cascade of attempted disciplining, appeals, disownments, and secession. Philadelphia Quarter attempted to "lay down" Green Street Meeting against its will, even though they had no power to do so. At issue was a problem of the authority of the elders, but it became conflated with a theological controversy between the followers of the historic Christ and the followers of the Inward Christ. The 1826 Yearly Meeting minutes recorded: "Time was allowed for Friends to sit a little together in silence after a short space of which our European Friends were alternately engaged in warning Friends to guard against submitting [to] a spirit of infidelity and unbelief in this day of trial, that all everywhere be particular to hold the doctrine of the benefits derived from the outward offering of Jesus Christ and of the outward blood that was shed upon the cross without the gates of Jerusalem and the outward sufferings and that all be careful to hold to the fullness of his Divinity and that in doctrine there can be no neutral ground…and if any hold otherwise there can be no religious fellowship with them." [xcvi] After a tense but inconclusive yearly meeting session, its elders moved toward setting up a committee to visit every monthly meeting to test the doctrinal soundness of their ministers and elders. The controversy was to be settled at the Yearly meeting the following year.

At the Philadelphia Yearly Meeting of 1827, the rural meetings attempted to even out the perceived imbalance of power by doubling the number of their representatives. This led to a deadlock between the evangelical clerk, Samuel Bettle, and the Quietist assistant clerk, John Comly. Reformers attempted to put Comly into the clerkship. After four days of shouting by both sides, Comly persuaded the liberals to withdraw to an evening gathering at Green Street, which led them to set up the framework of a second, parallel PYM. The Separation, which had been meant to be only temporary and at the level of the yearly meeting, forced each quarterly and monthly meeting to choose which yearly meeting they would recognize and led to what turned out to be a permanent division within almost every meeting. [xcvii]

Each side continued to refer to itself as Philadelphia Yearly Meeting, claiming it alone represented the authentic Quaker perspective and practice. The Orthodox position was that separatists (Hicksites) should be disowned as soon as possible, and that compromise with heretics was a betrayal of Christianity. Marriage between an Orthodox and a Hicksite was joining a Christian and an infidel.

13

Richland		left
Stroudsburgh		left
Bucks Quarter		
Buckingham		left
Plumstead	right	
Solebury		left
Wrightstown	right	
Middletown	right	
Fallsington	right	
Makefield	right	
Newtown		left
Concord		
Concord		left
Wilmington	right	
Birmingham		left
West Chester		left
Kennet – Western Q M	right	
Kennet Square Western Q M		left
Willistown	right	

The seating arrangement on the facing benches for ministers and elders at the Philadelphia Yearly Meeting held in 1826. The Plumstead contingent sat on the right side.

People who had worshipped in a meetinghouse all their lives were now threatened with eviction, and Hicksite pupils were expelled from Orthodox schools. The Hicksite position was that property should be divided along numerical lines, and since they comprised about 70 percent of the membership of Philadelphia Yearly Meeting, this position was advantageous to them. They disowned the Orthodox who were disowning them. There was a complete breakdown in communications, including disagreement as to what the issues were and the meanings of the words used to describe them. There was conflict about such fundamental ideas as the very structure of the Society and its statements of belief. The burial ground in Philadelphia, formerly used by all monthly meetings, was closed to those who did not recognize the authority of Philadelphia Orthodox Quarterly Meeting. When the Hicksites broke down part of the wall to build a new gate to gain access, the Orthodox had the perpetrators arrested and charged with trespass. [xcviii]Both sides attempted to gain vindication from other yearly meetings, and in the process precipitated divisions in Baltimore, New York, Ohio, and Indiana.

In hindsight it might be said that both sides contributed to the conflict. In becoming the guardians of tradition, the elders at times tended too strongly to repress the springing up of untraditional new life. [xcix]They went too far, judging and condemning those who were of a differing view, and were authoritarian in their attempt to impose as much uniformity in theology as they previously had in behavior. They seemed to have forgotten that Quaker decision making and governance were processes which included the entire body; instead of listening, they accused dissenters of "insubordination." The more liberal Friends erred in lacking forbearance, and the time honored waiting for "way to open." Instead of laboring with Orthodox Friends, they withdrew, stopped the dialogue, and left backbiting in its place. Ironically, they would later accuse minority Orthodox members who withdrew from majority Hicksite meetings as "violating the good order of the Society." Within a few months of the separation, Hicksites, afraid that the vocal Orthodox would disown them and seize their meetinghouses, escalated matters by controlling the meetinghouses first and changing the locks. They defensively proposed property division, which literally cemented the separation in place. Both sides seemed to have lost sight of the meeting for business as a spiritual experience dependent upon understanding hearts, gentleness, and a desire for unity. Both had lost sight of their common past as a Society grounded in love, and the shared work needed from them both.

Elias Hicks continued his ministry until the end of his life. A young Walt Whitman attended a sermon given by Hicks in 1829, a year before Hicks' death. Years later, Whitman described the scene: [c]

"Elias preaches anywhere--no respect of buildings—private or public houses, school-rooms, barns, even theatres—anything that will accommodate. This time is in a handsome ball-room, on Brooklyn Heights, overlooking New York....the second story of 'Morrison's Hotel,' used for the most genteel concerts, balls, and assemblies—a large cheerful, gay-color'd room, with glass chandeliers bearing myriads of sparkling pendants, plenty of settees and chairs held....all the principal dignitaries of the town. On a slightly elevated platform at the head of the room, facing the audience, sit a dozen or more Friends, most of them elderly, grim, and with their broad-brimmed hats on their heads. Three or four women, too, in their characteristic Quaker costumes and bonnets. All still as the grave.

At length after a pause and stillness becoming painful, Elias Hicks rises and stands for a moment or two without a word. A tall, straight figure, neither stout nor very thin, dressed in drab cloth, clean-shaved face, forehead of great expanse, and large and clear black eyes, long or middling long white hair; he was at this time between 80 and 81 years of age, his head still wearing the broad-brim. A moment looking around the audience with those piercing eyes, amid the perfect stillness. (I can almost see him and the whole scene now.) Then the words come from his lips, very emphatically and slowly pronounced, in a resonant, grave, melodious voice. "What is the chief end of Man?"...

Always Elias Hicks gives the service of pointing to the fountain of all naked theology, all religion, all worship, all the truth to which you are possibly eligible—namely yourself and your inherent relations. Others talk of Bibles, saints, churches, exhortations, vicarious atonements—the canons outside of yourself and apart from man--Elias Hicks to the religion inside of man's very own nature. This he incessantly labors to kindle, nourish, educate, bring forward and strengthen. He is the most democratic of the religionists—the prophets...

Of course what Elias promulg'd spread a great commotion among the Friends. Sometimes when he presented himself to speak in the meeting, there would be opposition—this led to angry words, gestures, unseemly noises, recriminations. Elias, at such times, was deeply affected—the tears rolled in streams down his cheeks—he silently waited the close of the dispute. "Let the Friend speak: let the Friend speak!" he would say when his supporters in the meeting tried to bluff off some violent orthodox person objecting to the new doctrinaire. But he never recanted."

VIGNETTE:

REGARDING ELIAS HICKS

"Friends were preserved in love and unity until Elias Hicks disturbed that harmony by lessening the Divine authenticity of the Holy Scripture, and then, when he supposed he had sufficiently prepared the minds of the people, he came out with his Unitarian principles or doctrine, and showed a wonderful fondness for speculation and reasoning, frequently asserting that he was not obliged to believe what our reason could not comprehend. Advice has been given him by some worthy Friends of New York Yearly Meeting, as well as those of other Yearly Meetings and from Europe, and have stated to him his sentiments relative to the divinity of Christ, which went to the destruction of the Christian religion and to produce divisions in [the] Society. But he has acquired a degree of obstinacy in which he is scarce equaled by any other man. It is owing to this that no advice that has been given him has been of any use. If Friends in Philadelphia should allow this man to visit families, and in this way spread his poisonous principles, divisions among them will assuredly be the consequences."

Excerpts from a letter by Thomas Eddy of New York to John Warder of Philadelphia, 1822.[ci]

CHAPTER FIVE:

PLUMSTEAD DIVIDED

PLUMSTEAD MEETING BEFORE THE SCHISM

For seventy years, Quaker life at Plumstead had continued with little change. There were, of course, the events concerning the American Revolution, and a minor increase in military disciplines during the War of 1812. Plumstead Meeting was optimistic about its future. In May 1824, Plumstead Preparative Meeting sent the following minute to Buckingham, "This meeting requests the Monthly Meeting to take into consideration the expediency of setting up a Monthly Meeting at Plumstead to be composed of that part of Buckingham Monthly Meeting which now constitutes Plumstead Preparative Meeting." [cii] Buckingham Monthly Meeting was supportive, but Bucks Quarterly Meeting was not.

The committee on the subject of settling a Monthly Meeting at Plumstead made the following report in writing viz. "We of the committee appointed to consider the propriety of setting up a Monthly Meeting at Plumstead to be composed of that part of the members of Buckingham Mo. meeting which now constitutes Plumstead Preparative Meeting, do agree to report, that having generally met and weightily considered the subject, are of the Judgment that the time hath nearly come that it would be right so to do—which we submit to the meeting."—

Saml. Wilson	Elizabeth Jones
James Shaw	Sarah Gillingham
John Good	Hannah Lancaster
James Bradshaw	Elizabeth Balderston
David Fell	Mary Johnson
Silas Preston	Elizabeth Pickering
Jeremiah Walton	Sarah Banes
Thomas Paxson	Hannah Kirkbride
John Brock	Elizabeth Carlisle
Cephas Ross	Deborah Brown
Dan. Carlisle	Edith Fell
Joseph Stradling	Massey Brock.—

and after deliberation thereon and the sentiments of Friends freely expressed, it appears to be the judgment of the meeting, that it will be right (the women's Meeting concurring therewith) to forward the proposal to the Quarterly meeting for its consideration and judgment.

The reply from BQM was that "way does not open with sufficient clearness to us to recommend the establishment of a monthly meeting at that place." [ciii] The reason was not given, but historically, of all of Buckingham's preparative meetings, Plumstead remained the weakest. There were several times when it failed to meet its financial quotas, and at one point Buckingham asked Friends "lying on that side of Buckingham Preparative Meeting toward Plumstead be excited to the pointings of duty in endeavoring to add strength to Plumstead Preparative Meeting." [civ]In addition, there was the issue of demographics. Plumstead, Solebury, and Buckingham Meetings were at the northern edge of the English Quaker population at a time when overall Quaker membership was declining. One purpose of the monthly meetings was to gather together several local congregations to unify and support one other. Solebury had established a monthly meeting early on, but as no new meetings formed in that area, it remained a monthly meeting of one. If Plumstead established its own monthly meeting, it and Buckingham would also have become solitary monthly meetings for the foreseeable future.

DIVISION COMES TO BUCKS QUARTER AND TO PLUMSTEAD: "LET US BURN HIM"

Buckingham Monthly Meeting's reply to the Yearly Meeting queries in February 1827 gave no indication of the turbulence that was to follow, responding with the usual: "Love and unity are maintained." But events had already been set in place that would soon radically change that. The Friends who had withdrawn from the April Philadelphia Yearly Meeting assembly and who had met at Green Street issued a printed address which stated in part: "A division exits among us developing in its progress averse to reconciliation. Doctrines held by one part of the Society of which we believe to be sound & edifying are pronounced by the other part to be unsound & spurious...

"Measures have been pursued which we deem oppressive…

"This blessed order has been infringed, both in the present Yearly Meeting, (producing in exampled disorder in some of its sittings) and in many of its subordinate branches, and has proved a fruitful source of the difficulties that now exist.

"It is under a solemn and deliberate view of this painful state of our affairs, that we feel bound to express to you, under a settled conviction of mind that the period has fully come in which we ought to look towards making a quiet retreat from this scene of confusion, and we therefore recommend to you deeply to weigh this momentous subject, and to adopt such a course as Truth, under solid and solemn deliberation may point to…"

Buckingham Friends reported that "after deliberate and solid consideration it is concluded to recommend it with our reports to the attention and consideration of the ensuing Quarterly Meeting." [cv]

A report read at Buckingham's June monthly meeting made by the Yearly Meeting representatives who had been sent by Bucks Quarter was even more dramatic in its assessment of the previous Philadelphia Yearly Meeting session:

"We the representatives appointed to attend the last Yearly Meeting agree to report: That from the unprecedented manner which the business of the said Yearly Meeting was conducted, we feel it to be our duty to inform the Quarterly Meeting, that amid great disorder, a Clerk was imposed on the meeting, contrary to the sense of the representatives and the meeting at large, and at the close a committee was appointed to visit the subordinate meetings, by the will of a party, over the heads of a large proportion of the meeting, and contrary to the solid sense of many; exercised brethren then expressed proceedings calculated to abridge our Christian privileges, and to lay waste all order and condescension in society.

"It is therefore our united judgement that it will be unsafe, by receiving such committee, reading the Extracts, or in any other manner to acknowledge the authority of the late Yearly Meeting." [cvi]

That same month, the Green Street (later called Hicksite) group met again, and sent out another epistle, which read in part:

"Those who oppose and condemn their brethren who may conscientiously differ from them in opinion, break the bond of Gospel fellowship.

"It is now about 5 years since [a desolating spirit] made its appearance in our hitherto favoured Society, so as to become a subject of general concern. For some time it was mostly confined to individuals acting as officers in the Church....Friends traveling in the ministry, with certificates from their Monthly and Quarterly meetings were interrupted in their labours. They were unjustly charged with preaching infidel doctrines, denying the divinity of Christ and undervaluing the Scriptures...It was not long, however, before the contagion spread. In the Monthly Meetings for Discipline measures of a party character were introduced...measures [which were] executed against the judgement and contrary to the voice of the larger part of Friends present.

"At Yearly Meeting means were recently taken therein to overrule the greater part of the representatives and a clerk was imposed upon the meeting."

They went on to propose to hold another Yearly Meeting in October.

Buckingham's response: "Buckingham very generally unites in recommending [the epistle] to the deliberate and weighty consideration of our next Quarterly Meeting." [cvii]

The Bucks Quarterly Meeting held August 30 was so acrimonious that some members thought it might be necessary to call in civil authorities.[cviii] The report from the Yearly Meeting representatives and the Green Street Epistle were read. All the monthly meetings united with it, and representatives were chosen to attend the Yearly Meeting set for October. This meeting was described in the Orthodox Quarterly minutes as follows:

Separatist [Hicksite] representatives to Yearly Meeting charged it of misconduct "without as we apprehend any just foundation, and concluded by stating it as their judgement that it would be unsafe to receive a committee which had been appointed by Yearly Meeting to visit the Quarterly and Monthly Meetings; or to read the extracts from the minutes from said Meeting; or in any other manner to acknowledge its authority... A printed [Hicksite] address was read proposing to establish another Meeting under the name of Philadelphia Yearly Meeting; this proposition was adopted and representatives appointed to attend the same. Thus completely dissolving the connection with and subordination to our Yearly Meeting, which has so long, and so beneficially, and so harmoniously existed. In which unpleasant situation no alternative presented to the Friends of good order and sound principles than to remain after the Separatists had withdrawn and continue Bucks Quarterly Meeting on its original foundation." A committee of Orthodox members was appointed to visit each of the monthly meetings, "to unite with them therein for the strength and assistance of those Meeting in the due support of our salutary order and Discipline." [23]

Separate publications, with obvious biases, existed for the Hicksite and Orthodox factions. A Hicksite publication described the same Quarterly Meeting events this way: "At the conclusion

[23] Bucks Quarterly Meeting minutes 31st d./8th mo./1827. Several pages of the minutes appear in the appendix.

of this meeting a request was made by an orthodox member of the Quarter, that those who did not unite with the measures that had been adopted would remain together at the rise of the meeting; and on some objection being made, "a distinguished minister" among the orthodox party, and a member of the Yearly Meeting committee, stated that nothing further was intended or designed, than to have a friendly conference together, upon which, Friends left the house. But the orthodox immediately appointed a clerk, and proceeded to open a meeting as Bucks Quarterly Meeting, although not one of the representatives from the Monthly Meetings stayed with them. This done, they adjourned till next day, when they again met; no measures being attempted by Friends to prevent them the use of the meeting-house. At this time, among other things, they appointed a committee to attend the Monthly Meetings." [cix]

Buckingham Monthly Meeting, held on September 3, 1827 was the first Monthly Meeting after the acrimonious Quarterly Meeting, and the Orthodox visitors were in attendance. The Monthly Meeting minutes recorded:

"A proposition having been made by a member for a few [Orthodox] Friends who are not in unity with this monthly meeting to remain in session for the purpose of holding Buckingham Monthly Meeting whose proposition being deliberately considered, and a free expression of sentiment taking place, the meeting very much unites in judgement that it would be altogether contrary and inconsistent with the discipline and practice of our religious society to grant or admit such a proposition. Notwithstanding which those individuals did, before this meeting concluded, nominate a clerk and proceed to transact business as a monthly meeting in opposition to this [one]." [cx]

A Hicksite publication added, "on the meeting being opened, [the Orthodox committee] offered a copy of the minute of their appointment.

The meeting, however, was unwilling to recognize their self-created powers, and declined the reading of their spurious document. The [committee] told Friends to leave the house, and permit them, the Orthodox present, to hold the Monthly Meeting, asserting, in opposition to the general body of Friends, that *they* were the meeting. Friends not consenting to leave the house, they without further ceremony appointed a clerk, and opened what they called Buckingham Monthly Meeting (with Hicksites refusing to withdraw and sitting among them) after which they adjourned to meet the following month at Plumstead [meetinghouse]. An Orthodox minister from England and another from Burlington Quarter were among the most active in these proceedings." [cxi] The Buckingham Monthly Meeting clerk was also the clerk of Buckingham Preparative Meeting, and was the caretaker of the Buckingham meetinghouse and graveyard. He had previously declared that he "had no unity with [Hicksites], nor their meetings," and had put a padlock on the graveyard gates.[cxii] Hicksite Friends were now getting worried that their meetinghouse also might be closed to them in the future.

The October Buckingham Monthly Meeting reported that an Orthodox Buckingham Preparative Meeting had been formed: "[List of names] have united and aided in opening and holding a preparative meeting (so called by them) in open violation of the good order established by this Society and in direct opposition to the sentiments of Friends generally expressed…" [cxiii]A Hicksite publication reported that the Preparative Meeting clerk, who had previously stated that he was not in unity with the Hicksite majority, was asked to step down. He ignored this request, and "Friends very generally expressed their disapprobation to his proceeding, but he did proceed, and went on reading the minutes of the previous Orthodox Monthly Meeting." Only one person encouraged him to continue, and he was seconded by a minister from England, who asserted that the prevailing sense was not the judgement of the meeting, but that it was "the conclusion of a few solid, weighty, Friends." [cxiv]

The conflict between the two bodies both calling themselves Buckingham Preparative Meeting was now about to get worse.

Although the Buckingham Monthly Meeting minutes appear very routine for the month of November, the Buckingham Preparative Meeting was chaotic. A Hicksite publication described the Buckingham Preparative Meeting opening with the Hicksites conducting business in the meetinghouse. The Orthodox men went to the carriage sheds and the women met in the balcony. A new caretaker was named by the Hicksites, and he proceeded to change the lock on a door. The trustees released the previous caretaker and asked for the keys to the woodshed. He refused to comply.

Meanwhile, about twenty Hicksites, along with a group of Orthodox members, refused to leave the meetinghouse. Evening was approaching and the meetinghouse was getting cold, so the Hicksites broke into the woodshed to get wood. Both groups had provisions made for spending the night in the meetinghouse. Between 8 and 9 o'clock, a man came to the door just as someone was leaving, and "in an angry and threatening manner, seized the [departing] young man by the collar. The door was immediately closed upon him, leaving one arm and leg between the doors; and the Friend was released from the grasp by a candle applied to the offending member... We take no pleasure in publishing these disgusting statements, they are both irksome and painful to us. But even Christian forbearance will justify our repelling slander with the weapons of truth." [cxv]

The same incident had also been described in the Orthodox publication: "The clerk stood by the table for a few moments, to see whether he would be permitted to proceed, but the [Hicksite clerk] persisted in retaining his seat, and read a minute opening a preparative meeting for the new sect.

It was then proposed by a Friend that they should quietly withdraw and hold their meeting out of the doors, as the followers of Elias Hicks seemed determined to preclude them from transacting the business in the house. This was accordingly done; for although the clerk of the preparative meeting had never been released, nor any other regularly appointed in his place, and the followers of Elias Hicks regardless of the discipline and order of the Society, had organized a new preparative meeting of a new sect, distinct from Friends, and of course could have no right, nor even a plausible excuse, for usurping the control and possession of the property; yet Friends patiently submitted to the wrong, and did not contend with them, even for what was so evidently their just right. The new preparative meeting appointed another person to take possession of the house… who began to take off the lock while the meeting was yet sitting, and accomplished the task before they broke up. He came back with a new lock, which he fastened on the door; after which he nailed down the window sashes. The women, and some of the men, went away, but about twenty men remained to guard the premises. By this time the stoves had gotten quite cool, and more fire was wanted. They demanded the key of the woodhouse from the Friend who had charge of the property, but he declined. They immediately went to the woodhouse and broke it open. Evening was now approaching, and they began to make preparations for passing the night in the meetinghouse: A basket of victuals and some bedclothes were brought to them by their friends. These extraordinary and disgraceful proceedings spread quickly through the neighborhood…The [caretaker] became ashamed to be seen there, lest he should be considered accessory to them, so he left between 8 and 9 o'clock in the evening. Some time after he had left the house, a Friend passing along the road, supposing the caretaker was still there, stopped to speak with him. He opened the door, and stepped upon the threshold, when several of the noisy tenants ran to him, and pushing the door with violence, caught him by one leg and one arm, between it and the half which remained closed. While in this predicament, one of the persons in the house called out "bring a candle and let us burn him!" He was, however, aware of their design and extinguished the candle. The followers of Elias Hicks remained in the house that night, and we are informed, the next night also. It is with feelings of regret and shame that we record these most disgraceful transactions." [cxvi]

Division had reached Plumstead Meeting as well. The Orthodox minutes reported, "At Plumstead the like spirit of insubordination to and disregard of the discipline of our religious society appeared in many of the members, the clerk being of that number. They rejected the committees of both the Quarterly and Monthly Meetings that are subordinate to our ancient Yearly Meeting and refusing to read their minutes of appointment and no opening appearing in either end of the House to proceed without great interruption, Friends withdrew and transacted their business on the Meeting lands, the women at the horse blocks and the men in the carriage sheds.

"In reviewing the state of those Meetings although there is a considerable number of Friends in each standing as we fully believe faithfully attached to and desirous of supporting the order and discipline of our religious society, yet such is the disposition manifested by the separatists that we cannot indulge the hope that by the time of holding our next preparative meeting, Friends will be permitted to transact the business of them in their respective meetinghouse with that tranquil solemnity which is desirable in deliberating on those important subjects that will then necessarily come before those meetings." [cxvii]

Bucks Quarterly Meeting made an enumeration of all its members in 1827, with notations as to whether the person was leaning Orthodox, Hicksite, or neutral. Plumstead at the time of separation had

287 members (including minors). Of these, 41 adults and 18 minors declared themselves as Orthodox Friends, with the remaining 228 members declaring themselves Hicksite or neutral.

Buckingham reported that six-sevenths of their membership was Hicksite. [cxviii] Philadelphia Yearly Meeting requested an inventory and description of property, books, and records that had remained in the hands of Hicksites. Buckingham Monthly Meeting reported the following: Buckingham Preparative Meeting: thirty acres, a meetinghouse, a school, a burying ground and two additional small lots with schools; Solebury: three acres, a meetinghouse, burying ground, plus two additional lots, one with a school; Wrightstown: five acres, a meetinghouse, burying ground, plus a lot with a tenant house and two schoolhouse lots; Plumstead: fifteen acres, a meetinghouse, and burying ground, valued at $2,000. [cxix]

The division led to a host of other conflicts: over the title of the meetinghouse lands, over money, (particularly restricted funds that had been a bequest to the meeting); over the books which recorded the births, deaths and marriages of members, over the minutes of the business meetings, and over the current certificates for traveling Friends. [cxx]

DECLINE

A consistent decline in membership, which had already begun due to seventy years of disownments, now accelerated at Plumstead. Twenty percent of its membership had been lost with the schism, including many of its elders. These Quakers established an Orthodox Plumstead Meeting which met nearby (see vignette).

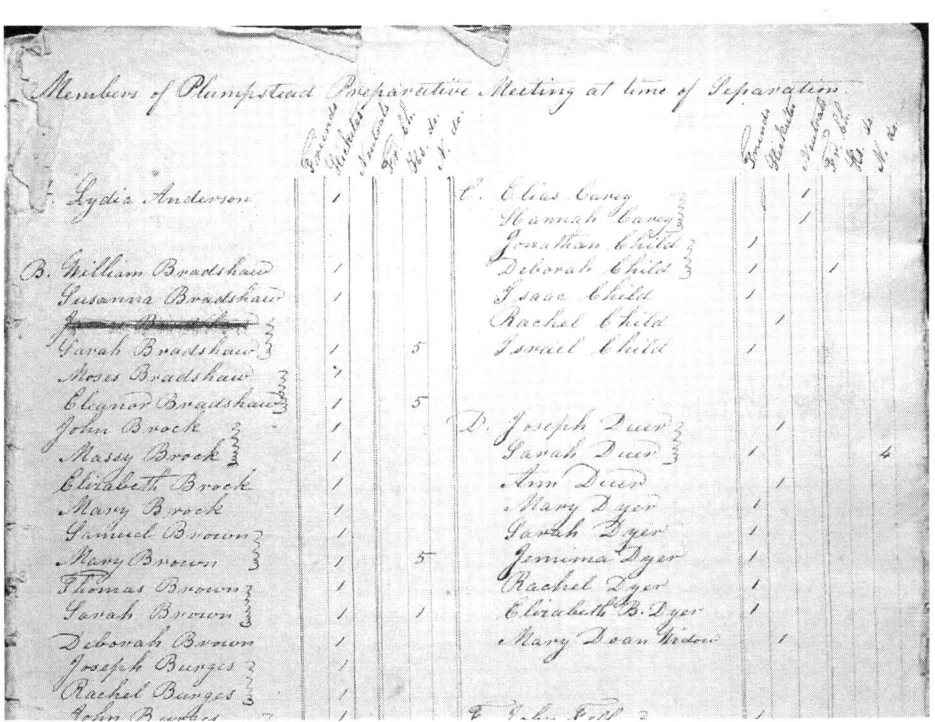

Members of Plumstead Preparative Meeting at time of Separation

	Name	Friends	Hicksites	Neutrals	Fr. Ch.	Hi. do.	N. do.
A.	Lydia Anderson		1				
B.	William Bradshaw		1				
	Susanna Bradshaw		1				
	~~[illegible]~~						
	Sarah Bradshaw		1			5	
	Moses Bradshaw		1				
	Eleanor Bradshaw		1			5	
	John Brock		1				
	Massy Brock		1				
	Elizabeth Brock		1				
	Mary Brock		1				
	Samuel Brown		1				
	Mary Brown		1			5	
	Thomas Brown		1				
	Sarah Brown		1			1	
	Deborah Brown		1				
	Joseph Burges		1				
	Rachel Burges		1				
	John Bu[illegible]		1				

	Name	Friends	Hicksites	Neutrals	Fr. Ch.	Hi. do.	N. do.
C.	Elias Carey			1			
	Hannah Carey			1			
	Jonathan Child	1					
	Deborah Child	1			1		
	Isaac Child	1					
	Rachel Child		1				
	Israel Child	1					
D.	Joseph Duer		1				
	Sarah Duer	1					4
	Ann Duer		1				
	Mary Dyer	1					
	Sarah Dyer	1					
	Jemima Dyer	1					
	Rachel Dyer	1					
	Elizabeth B. Dyer	1					
	Mary Doan Widow		1				
E.	John Fell	1					

A partial list of Plumstead members in 1827, indicating whether they were Hicksite, Orthodox, or neutral. The full list appears in the appendix.

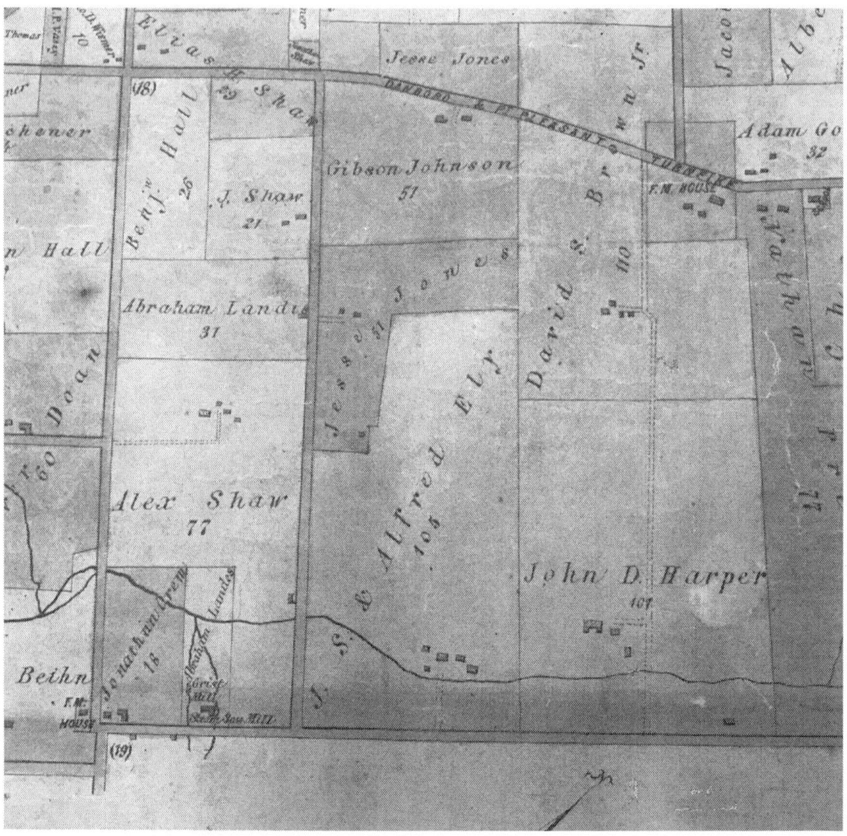

A map of Plumstead farmland in 1859, showing the Hicksite meetinghouse in the upper right and the orthodox meetinghouse in the lower left, separated by a distance of about 2 ½ miles.

Then, in 1835, a petition was sent to Buckingham to grant the establishment of a meeting in Doylestown for "those residing in the village." [cxxi] Several of those signing were Plumstead members, and over time, the membership at Doylestown Meeting grew, in this town that had now become the county seat. Perhaps more significant was the financial prosperity of the new meeting. A brick meetinghouse was nearly complete and mostly paid for within nine months of Doylestown's inception as an indulged meeting. [cxxii]

Plumstead Township was increasing in population, but a substantial portion of the newer inhabitants were of German descent and of the Mennonite religion. Nearby farms of this period, on Valley Park Road and on Durham Road are named the Kraut-Chittick, Overholt-Myer, Leidy Myer, Shaddinger, Fretz, Pfeiffer, and Bewighouse Farms, all of German derivation. [cxxiii] By the end of the nineteenth century, German descendants comprised the majority of the residents of Plumstead Township. Matthews attributed the influx to "the addiction of Mennonites to agriculture rather than to mercantile or professional pursuits, and Plumstead has remained an agricultural township, with no large villages." [cxxiv]

A spirit of malaise now infused the Quaker minutes. Several times in the 1830s the Buckingham Monthly Meeting minutes stated that love and unity "does not appear to be generally maintained," or "does not prevail as extensively as it ought to be." [cxxv] In the 1840s, the Quarterly Meetings were said to be attended in a crowded, disorderly manner. And in 1852, Buckingham submitted the following notice to the public newspapers:

"The increasing attendance of a large concourse of people upon our grounds, both male and female, who are not members, during the sittings of our Quarterly Meetings, having been a subject of much dissatisfaction for many years has again claimed our serious consideration and in order that these meetings hereafter may not be subjected to such great interruption, we deem it right to give public notice that our Quarterly Meetings, when at Buckingham, are held exclusively for members of the Society, and we consider it an imposition and a violation of good order for others to attend them, or to collect upon our premises for the object of social amusement and diversion.

"We believe that most of those who have been present at some of the occasions alluded to, are fully sensible of the necessity of at once terminating a practice, so much at variance with the objects of a religious meeting and reproachful to anybody of professing Christians.

"There are, nevertheless, those who would wish to accommodate such of their families as are members, but the numbers of these being comparatively small and composed of orderly individuals (they remaining quietly upon our premises during the sitting of the Meeting) has not been the occasion of the dissatisfaction.

"We wish it also distinctly understood that trafficking in any kind of refreshments whatsoever will not be permitted." [cxxvi]

Although the minutes in the 1850s were recording "the condition of the neglect of the attendance of our Meetings having claimed our attention," [cxxvii] Hicksite Friends were introducing more tolerance and creativity into their Quakerism. Unlike earlier times, the Buckingham minutes now recorded instances when a member who had married someone "not a Friend" was permitted to continue as a member of the Society. Ministers and elders were being rejected, leaving the facing benches depopulated, and at some meetinghouses, men and women's business meetings were held jointly. [cxxviii]

With a declining membership, maintenance of the building and grounds was becoming an issue. In 1854, a stone wall was erected around the Plumstead Meeting burying ground, paid for by subscriptions. The local newspaper noted, "We are glad to see a disposition manifested in the Society of Friends to improve their property, and especially to protect their burying grounds, and keep them in better order than many of them have been for years past. " [cxxix] The following year, a small, (approx. 18' x 24') two-story caretaker's house was built on the meetinghouse grounds.[24]

[24] Plumstead Meeting minutes, (provided to Laura Fell by Comly Michener) recorded in March 1855, that "as schools are now made public by Government, there was a proposal made in this meeting to use the money of the General Subscription Fund for Use of Schools, through the erecting of a dwelling on the Meeting property, with which the meeting unites and Abraham Michener and Aaron Burgess were

Photo by Alan D. Gray

appointed to supervise the building thereof." The cost of the construction was $525.10, most of the work being done by members. (Fell, p. 7) This is reflected in tax records of the time. In 1855, Plumstead Meeting paid both county and state taxes on ten acres of "unseated" land, with the remaining five acres, presumably including the meetinghouse, being completely untaxed. In 1856, the ten acres changed to a "seated" category, (meaning the land was used as a place of residence and occupied), and the value per acre doubled. A copy of the 1859 tax record appears in the appendix. The decision to build the house seems wise, especially in light of declining membership. The occupant of the house could contribute to the meeting either through caretaking services or by paying rent, and having someone living on the property might have helped serve as a deterrent to vandalism. Today the house is owned by Buckingham Friends Meeting; it is occupied and in good repair.

Despite this improvement in the maintenance and security of the property, grave robbers attacked the Plumstead burial grounds the following year.

Notice to Trespassers.

ALL those persons who, regardless of law and good order, recently trespassed on the premises of the Society of Friends of Plumstead, by abruptly driving into the Grave Yard with wagon and horses, disfiguring some of the graves, and opening others, and disinterring several corpses, and taking them away without consent of the Sexton or any of the Trustees, are hereby requested to come forward and render satisfaction for the same without delay, which may save cost, prevent exposure, and oblige the undersigned.

ABRAHAM MICHENER, } Committee
THOMAS STRADLING, } of Trust.
DAVID CARR, Sexton.

Plumstead, 8th month 26th, 1856.–3t

N. B.—Notice is also hereby given to all other persons not to commit the like depredations.

A census of the Plumstead membership in 1862 (see appendix) recorded thirty-four male adults, forty female adults, and nineteen minors, for a total of ninety-three members. They also noted twenty-eight additional nonmember minors, where only one parent was a member. [cxxx] In thirty-five years, Plumstead had been reduced to one-third of its former size. There were times in the next couple of years when meeting for worship went unattended, and in 1864, Plumstead reported to the Monthly Meeting that the midweek and preparative meetings were so small that they believed the time had come to discontinue these meetings. The Quarterly Meeting rejected their request. Five years later, Plumstead requested again to have the midweek meetings laid down. This time the Quarter responded: ".after deliberate consideration united with by the meeting, the women's meeting also uniting therein, the said meeting is therefore discontinued and the members attached to Buckingham Preparative Meeting. [cxxxi]The list of names transferred to Buckingham Meeting 6th mo./7th d./ 1869, totaled eighty-two. [cxxxii]

The following is a copy of a minute in relation to Plumstead Meeting received from our Quarterly Meeting

"To Buckingham Monthly Meeting of Friends,

Plumstead Meeting. At Bucks Quarterly Meeting of Friends held at Wrightstown 2nd Mo 25th 1869
" The matter as contained in the report from
" Buckingham Monthly Meeting was after deliberate
" Consideration united with by the Meeting, Women's
" Meeting also uniting therein, the said Meeting
" is therefor discontinued and the members attached

203.

" to Buckingham Preparative Meeting, the clerks
" were directed to forward information thereof to
" Buckingham Monthly Meeting

Extracted from the minutes

By Barclay Knight
Rachel Palmer } Clerks "

VIGNETTE:

PLUMSTEAD ORTHODOX MEETING

This drawing of the Plumstead Orthodox Meetinghouse was based upon the memory of one who had seen it. Courtesy of the Friends Historical Library

The Orthodox Friends of Plumstead, "being rejected and much opposition offered" within the Plumstead Meetinghouse, again met outdoors on meetinghouse grounds in October 1827. In November, as cold weather set in, they met in the nearby home of Jesse Jones, [25] and in later months at the home of John Fell.

Page 5
Last to fix on a scite for Building a meeting
house, Report that most of them met and
agreed on a place near where the meeting is
now held on the land of Joseph Dyer which
can be had for that purpose
John Fell and Daniel C Rich are appointed
a Committee to solicite subscriptions in aid of
purchasing a lot of ground and the erection of
a Meeting-house thereon for the accommodati-
:on of the society of Friends Commonly called Quakers
The Meeting Concludes

In April 1836, they purchased sixty perches of land on Landisville Road from Joseph Dyer, contiguous with the land of John Fell,[cxxxiii] with the intention of building a meetinghouse. The one-story frame meetinghouse was completed by September 1837 [cxxxiv] at a cost of $550.00. [cxxxv]

[25] Buckingham Orthodox Monthly Meeting minutes 5th d./ 11th mo./1827. Meanwhile, Buckingham Orthodox Monthly Meeting conducted its business meetings on Mondays in the Plumstead Hicksite meetinghouse until March of 1828, when they "found the meetinghouse closed against them and having received information that the separatists would not suffice it to be opened, they retired [to the home of John Fell] (Buckingham Orthodox Monthly Meeting Minutes 3rd d./3rd mo./1828).

Plumstead Orthodox Preparative Friends established a fund for the schooling of poor children and created a library in the meeting-house. They had the use of any of the Friends schools and the Plumstead Hicksite burying ground, subject to Hicksite control.[cxxxvi] However, over time, as the effect of the decades of disownments was felt, all of the small Orthodox congregations that comprised Buckingham Orthodox Monthly Meeting slowly declined.

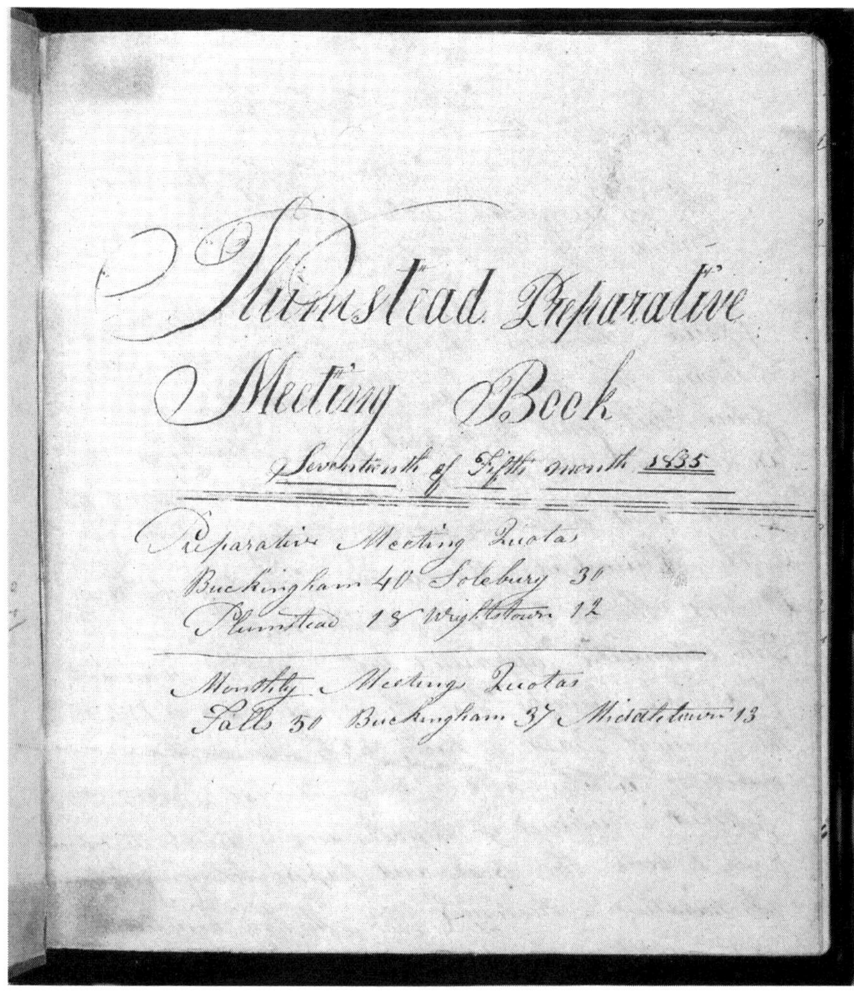

Plumstead Preparative Meeting Book

Seventeenth of Fifth month 1835

Preparative Meeting Quotas
Buckingham 40 Solebury 30
Plumstead 18 Wrightstown 12

Monthly Meeting Quotas
Falls 50 Buckingham 37 Middletown 13

In 1847, Buckingham Monthly Meeting formed a committee to visit the preparative meetings, owing to their "striped" conditions. The solution, they felt, was that Friends needed to "Know our proper place and station in the church" and to be "more willing to leave the cumbering things of this world and sit with each other in the middle of the week." [cxxxvii]

Despite the committee's efforts, the congregations that constituted Buckingham Orthodox Monthly Meeting gradually became defunct. Solebury Orthodox Preparative Meeting was laid down in 1857, and Wrightstown in 1869. In May of 1878, Plumstead Orthodox Preparative Meeting was finally laid down, and its books and papers were transferred to Buckingham Orthodox Preparative Meeting.[cxxxviii]

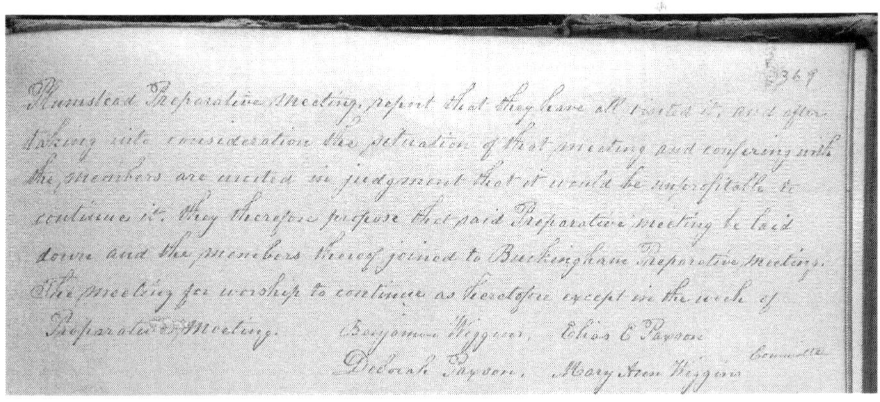

369

Plumstead Preparative Meeting, report that they have all visited it, and after taking into consideration the situation of that meeting and conferring with the members are united in judgment that it would be unprofitable to continue it. they therefore propose that said Preparative meeting be laid down and the members thereof joined to Buckingham Preparative Meeting. The meeting for worship to continue as heretofore except in the week of Preparative Meeting. Benjamin Wiggins, Elias E Paxson, Deborah Paxson, Mary Ann Wiggins Committee

A new roof was put on the meetinghouse in November of that year,[cxxxix] but in time, the land reverted back to its original owner, [cxl]and shortly before 1900[cxli] the vacant meetinghouse was demolished. Daniel Rich was the last member of Plumstead Orthodox Meeting, sometimes attending alone. He survived the closing of the meetinghouse, and after his demise, was interred in the Plumstead Hicksite burying ground.

CHAPTER SIX:

CHANGES IN QUAKER CULTURE AND THEOLOGY FROM THE CIVIL WAR INTO THE TWENTIETH CENTURY

Both the Hicksite and the Orthodox Friends were characterized by immobility in the decades following the schism of 1827. Early on, introspective quietists were in the majority of both groups, but by the end of this period, the liberal element had taken over the Hicksites, and was increasing among the Orthodox. A desire to preserve traditions was replaced by an effort to find ways to respond to the world, such as participating in reform organizations and political lobbying. [cxlii] There were, as well, cultural changes in speech, dress, architecture, and the structure of Quaker leadership. This is the story of that transformation.

ENGAGEMENT WITH OUTSIDE ORGANIZATIONS OVER SLAVERY LEADS TO RE-EVALUATION OF THE PEACE TESTIMONY AND AN EMPHASIS ON INDIVIDUAL CONSCIENCE

The peace testimony was a deeply felt Quaker value which was more important than the loss of political power during the French and Indian War and was worth the persecution endured by the Society during the American Revolution. During the self-reflective Quietist period, the insight that slavery was an inherently violent institution became widespread among Friends. Quakers worked to emancipate their own slaves and were concerned for the education and welfare of the freed, but in dealing with American society as a whole, there was a question as to how to engage with others in accordance with Friends' principles. While Quakers such as Thomas Garrett and Lucretia Mott were outspoken abolitionists outside the meetinghouse, the majority of Hicksite and Orthodox Friends in the 1840s would have argued that the rhetoric and political activities of the abolitionists were the product of an enthusiasm that was unQuakerly, and was more likely to lead to war than to the end of slavery. [cxliii]

In time, it became apparent that slavery in society was not going to be dislodged peacefully, and the dilemma then became: How much support for coercion and violence could be justified in order to abolish another kind of violence? As Friends began to participate in outside organizations that were in sympathy with their causes, they were forced to come to terms with the extensive demands of the beliefs they had developed.[cxliv]

By the 1860s, both the Hicksite and Orthodox factions struggled with the war, slavery, and identity, and both tried to remain inside their insulated communities while simultaneously being tempted by outside factors. Each branch of the Society of Friends possessed, to differing degrees, an elderly and respected leadership who prized introspective Quietist morality, and who distrusted outside organizations for their potentially corrosive impact upon young Friends. [cxlv] The younger generation, however, remained more attracted to the energy and idealism of the abolitionist organizations, and were more likely to embrace change and activism in all contexts. Powers argues that the most serious problem of this period was that of a generational divide, precipitated by the emergence of the nonsectarian abolitionist movement. (See Vignette: Quaker Contributions during the Civil War).

Comparing the two Philadelphia Yearly Meetings, however, it is evident that the Hicksite Yearly Meeting was the more creative and dynamic body, in which hardly a year went by without the introduction of some new concept. In membership, they outnumbered the Orthodox two to one. There were a multitude of committees dealing with a number of focused concerns, and visitors and communications from outside Yearly Meeting were frequently entertained.

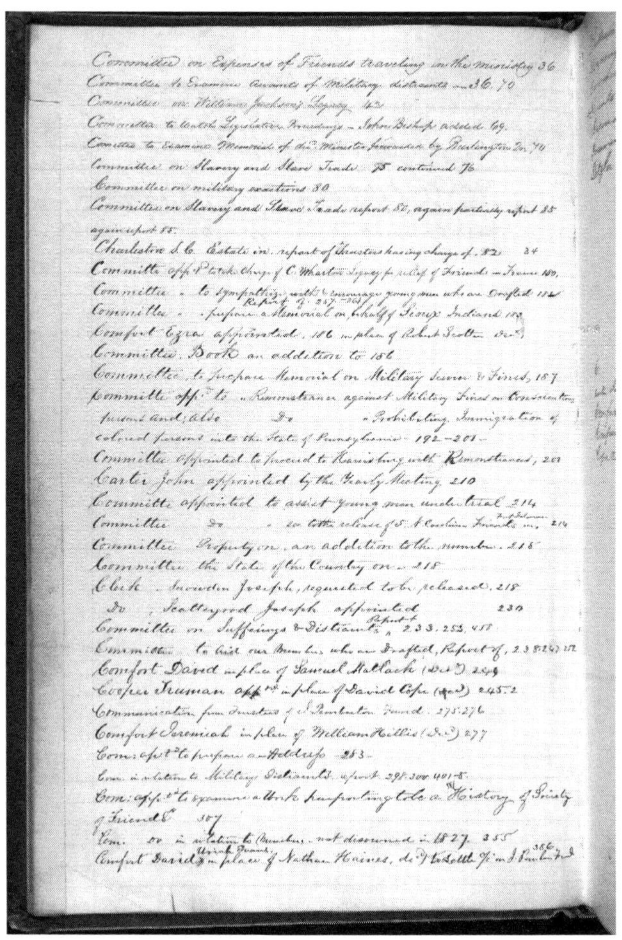

Committee on Expenses of Friends traveling in the ministry 36
Committee to Examine Accounts of Military distraints — 36. 70
Committee on William Jackson's Legacy 42
Committee to Watch Legislative Proceedings — John Bishop added 69.
Committee to Examine Memorial of dec.d Minister forwarded by Burlington Qr. 70
Committee on Slavery and Slave Trade 75 continued 76
Committee on military exactions 80
Committee on Slavery and Slave Trade report 80, again partially report 85
again report 85.
Charleston S. C. Estate in. report of Trustees having charge of. 82 84
Committee app.d to take charge of C. Wharton Legacy for relief of Friends in France 180,
Committee .. to sympathize with & encourage young men who are Drafted 184
Report of. 257–264
Committee .. prepare a Memorial on behalf of Sioux Indians 185
Comfort Ezra appointed. 186 in place of Robert Scotton Dec.d
Committee. Book an addition to 186
Committee to prepare Memorial on Military Service & Fines, 187
Committee app.d to .. Remonstrance against Military Fines on Conscientious
persons and; also Do .. Prohibiting Immigration of
colored persons into the State of Pennsylvania 192–201
Committee Appointed to proceed to Harrisburg with Remonstrances, 201
Carter John appointed by the Yearly Meeting 210
Committee appointed to assist young man under trial 214
Committee Do .. [illegible] release of S. N. Carolina Friends [illegible] 214
Committee Property on. an addition to the number. 215
Committee the State of the Country on .. 218
Clerk .. Snowden Joseph, requested to be released. 218
Do , Scattergood Joseph appointed 230
Committee on Sufferings & Distraints, Report 233. 253. 458
Committee to visit our Members who are Drafted, Report of, 238 247 252
Comfort David in place of Samuel Mattlack (Dec.d) 244
Cooper Truman app.td in place of David Cope (dec.d) 245. 2
Communication from Trustees of I. Pemberton Fund. 275. 276
Comfort Jeremiah in place of William Hillis (Dec.d) 277
Com: app.td to prepare an Address 283
Com. in relation to Military Distraints. report 298. 300. 401–5.
Com: app.d to examine a Work purporting to be a History of Society
of Friends &c 307
Com. .. in relation to Members .. not disowned in 1827. 355
Comfort David [illegible] in place of Nathan Haines, dec.d to settle [illegible] 386

Hicksites sent more petitions to those in government about the need for reforms than the Orthodox Friends and appeared to be more involved with the non-Quaker world than the parallel body. [cxlvi]

Hicksites, generally more rural and geographically removed from Yearly Meeting oversight than their Orthodox brethren, were already more disposed towards acting outside the loose constraints of their leadership. The widespread embrace of abolitionist sentiments on the part of Hicksite Friends, combined with a vigorous rereading and dissection of the Bible, (a major point of emphasis in contemporary articles in the *Friends Intelligencer*), resulted in a general reevaluation of the peace testimony on the part of many, causing what some Hicksites would call "a period of chaos." Sympathies with abolition explain not only why more Hicksite Friends fought in the war than Orthodox Friends, but also why Hicksite Friends were not as strict in disowning soldiers who refused to acknowledge their error in fighting—they even retained a brigadier general in their membership after the war. [cxlvii] This may not have been a huge leap, however, as Hicksites prided themselves on being tolerant of the views of others, and placed a high premium on individual conscience. [cxlviii]

A LOSS OF CONSENSUS CONTRIBUTES TO GREATER TOLERANCE

From the beginning of Quakerism there existed a system of carefully balanced emphases: inner light versus scripture, inward reflection versus outward action, individual conscience versus group authority. Strict conformity could be maintained as long as members, or at least the influential leadership, could agree on what constituted the truth. As various groups began to simplify versions of their faith, polarization and conflict developed. In the 1820s, Philadelphia Friends made the traumatic discovery that the eighteenth-century consensus had vanished and could not be refashioned.

The schism did immense harm to Philadelphia Yearly Meeting and diluted the impact of Friends on American society. Virtually all Quakers were continuing to press for indigenous rights, temperance, pacifism, and legal equality for Blacks. They were pleading for moderation, gradual reform, and respect, but unfortunately, everyone could see that Quakers did not practice towards one another what they advocated to everyone else.

Not all had been lost, however. The Orthodox had a Quietist majority and evangelical minority, whereas the Hicksites had a Quietist majority and a liberal minority. Visitors to a local meeting would have had a difficult time knowing which camp they were experiencing. As time went by, Hicksite and Orthodox Friends worked together on common causes and even visited one another's meetings. Friends learned to live with, respect, and even love individuals with whom they had profound differences. Such tolerance of diversity contributed to the birth of modern Quakerism.[cxlix]

THE RISE OF SCIENCE AND URBANIZATION IMPACTS QUAKER THOUGHT

Howard Brinton points out that the rise of science as a source of truth also impacted Quakerism during the late 1800s. In the past, reason had been considered a reliable guide to moral and religious truth if illuminated by the inner light and checked by the New Testament. Social service was always held to be essential in Christian behavior provided it arose from divine leading. There was, however, a gradual change toward secularization, leading many Quakers to become more intellectual and humanitarian in outlook. This was accelerated in the Society of Friends by higher education. A rapid increase in the application of science had given man an extraordinary control over nature, and reliance on the Divine seemed less essential. In earlier generations, most Friends were farmers; now many were living in cities or suburbs where the mysterious and unpredictable aspects of creation appeared at a minimum.[cl]

CHANGES IN QUAKER CULTURE

The concern for a peculiar, distinctive identity decreased during the last half of the nineteenth century. As the numbers of Friends declined, plainness in speech and dress became less about signaling group identity and more about moderation. The practice of wearing plain clothing began to wane after 1840, especially among the young, but official rejection of plainness by the Yearly Meetings took another fifty years. [cli]

An antique bonnet on display in the Plumstead Meetinghouse

The movement away from uniformity had repercussions inside the meetinghouse as well. As trust in the individual conscience increased, the role of ministers, elders and overseers gradually diminished. During the first quarter of the twentieth century, liberal Friends ended the practice of recording spiritual gifts and resorted to appointing people to committees to carry out the work of the meeting. The "elder" designation fell away, replaced by "weighty" Friends whose gifts did not set them apart from others. A rejection of the spiritual gifts [of ministers] led to the understanding that equality of all people precludes such recognition. [clii]The Chestnut Hill meetinghouse, built in 1931, was the first in Philadelphia Yearly Meeting to be constructed without facing benches, a physical manifestation of the programmatic change that had occurred.

What became modern Quaker thought was arising due to several factors. Consensus among Quakers and Quaker leaders had vanished during the period of the schism, and what had taken its place was an emphasis on individual conscience and toleration of differences. Over successive generations, the old bitterness generated by the schism gave way to a collective effort in shared causes, such as prison reform, the temperance movement, and the rights of women. In the Delaware Valley, Friends from both branches established the Friends Historical Association and created the John Woolman Memorial site in New Jersey. By the early twentieth century, a new spirit seemed to prevail, which would eventually lead to the healing of the schism. British Friends had already taken a liberal turn, and in fact, one of the most important events in the emergence of modern liberal Quakerism was the Manchester Conference in 1895.[cliii] In America, under the inspiration of Rufus Jones and others, a new teaching ministry developed, tasked with helping the Society of Friends through the difficulties created by modern thought. It was discovered that, because Quakerism is based on immediate experience, it had little to fear from the inroads of scientific or historical research. Early Quaker history and thought which had become obscured and distorted by the conflicts of the nineteenth century began to be readily available in books and periodicals. [cliv] Quakers were rediscovering what their ancestors had known, that the love of one another is at the heart of the Christian message. [clv]

VIGNETTE:

THE QUAKER EXPERIENCE DURING THE CIVIL WAR

The Peace Testimony, a commitment to nonviolence based on the belief that all human beings contain that of the Divine, constrained many young Friends from participating in the war. As a result, some were arrested and imprisoned for refusing to serve. Those who did join the military risked expulsion from the Society of Friends, and heartbreaking division within their families.

Despite the potential for discipline and disownment, the minutes of Buckingham Monthly Meeting were surprisingly silent when it came to the Civil War, especially in comparison to both the French and Indian War and the American Revolution. For example, the agenda for August, 1863, just a few weeks after the battle of Gettysburg was as follows: 1) Representatives were chosen to attend the next Quarterly meeting; 2) the 1st, 2nd, and 8th queries were responded to; 3) names were brought forward for the next clerk of the monthly meeting. The Bucks Quarterly minutes were equally silent; however, the minutes for the Philadelphia Yearly Meeting for Sufferings contained much wartime advice. [clvi]

Individual Friends sought to abolish slavery in a variety of ways. Some appealed to the moral conscience of those who held slaves, while others refused to purchase goods procured by slave labor. Still others established antislavery organizations that distributed abolitionist newspapers and pamphlets. Participation in the Underground Railroad, made illegal by the Fugitive Slave Law of 1850, was a direct, although risky, means of assistance.

Another mode of abolition was in lobbying state and federal governments to adopt antislavery legislation. Quakers famously visited President Lincoln and Secretary of War Stanton many times, both as individuals and in groups.

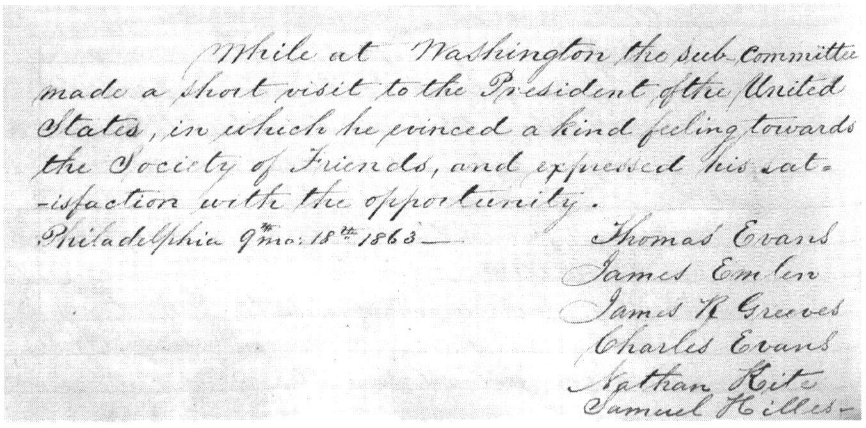

While at Washington the sub-Committee made a short visit to the President of the United States, in which he evinced a kind feeling towards the Society of Friends, and expressed his satisfaction with the opportunity.

Philadelphia 9th mo: 18th 1863—

Thomas Evans
James Emlen
James R Greeves
Charles Evans
Nathan Kite
Samuel Hilles—

Their impact upon officials was felt in four ways:

1. By discussing the concept that in improving the welfare of others, humans may be acting as instruments of Divine Will.
2. By persuading officials of the desirability of universal emancipation over gradual movements toward ending slavery.
3. By arguing for the creation of a conscientious objector status to enabled men to serve in a noncombatant role (the need for such a classification became particularly acute after the 1863 conscription law).

4. By indicating concern for the relief and education of freed peoples, resulting in the creation of the Freedmen's Bureau. [clvii]

CHAPTER SEVEN:

PLUMSTEAD MOVES TOWARD MODERN TIMES

THE REBUILDING OF THE PLUMSTEAD MEETINGHOUSE

Although Plumstead Preparative Meeting had been laid down and its members attached to Buckingham Preparative Meeting, Quakers were still gathering regularly at the Plumstead Meetinghouse as an indulged group. There was interest in getting the property in better shape, and the hope of attracting new members. The Buckingham minutes of 1874 report: "At the request of a member of Plumstead branch of our meeting, [a committee was] appointed to examine our property at that place and to make such recommendation regarding it as the circumstances of the case may seem to require." [clviii]The *Doylestown Intelligencer* further stated, "This house is now very old, and as the meeting is small and unable to bear much expense the property is much out of repair and can hardly be considered a comfortable place of meeting," as well as the hope that "when the house is put in good order the interest in the meeting in the vicinity will be increased." [clix]

The committee reported six months later that it was united in repairing the Plumstead meetinghouse, and that most of the work could be financed by selling the woodland north of the Point Pleasant turnpike. The five acres that were sold paid for a little over half of the final expense.

The renovation was actually a complete rebuilding, which took place in 1875. The building's height was reduced from two stories to one, and by some accounts it was also shortened at the east end. Hiram Michener sent a team of horses to help with the work. [26]During the construction, meeting for worship was discontinued at Plumstead from July until November, and Plumstead Friends attended either Buckingham or Doylestown meetings. [clx]

On completion of the work, the Friends tasked with auditing the accounts of the Plumstead Building Committee reported in writing as follows:

"The Friends appointed to audit the accounts of the building committee for Plumstead meeting house have attended to the duties assigned them, having examined their vouchers and found them correct. The whole cost of rebuilding being one thousand three hundred and eight dollars and thirteen cents. The building committee have collected from real estate sold seven hundred and fifty dollars.

	$750.00
Old lumber and stone sold	$ 93.24
Donations	$17.00
Making eight hundred sixty four dollars and 24 cents.	$ 864.24

This amount has been paid over for materials found and to the contractor, leaving a balance yet unpaid of $447.89."

[26] Shaddinger, p. 20. She also reports that "according to the old markers the present building is not as large as the one built in 1752."

The meeting accepted this report and directed that the unpaid balance be satisfied from the sale of wood from the premises of Buckingham Meeting. [clxi] An account of the expenses involved included the names of the contractors and the cost of the date stone and a stove. It was labor of love, with much of the hauling of materials and grading done at no charge by meeting members. [clxii]A celebratory photograph was taken at its completion.

The Plumstead Meetinghouse in 1875. To the right are Nathan Preston and wife, who lived next door to the meetinghouse. In the center are Mrs. Michener and child.

The design of the renovated meetinghouse was very much in keeping with the times. The colonial single-cell style was coming back into favor as an adjustment to the smaller Friends congregations. Joint business meetings of men and women were gaining momentum in the 1870s, making the dividing wooden partition unnecessary. At Plumstead, a portion of that partition was recycled into wainscoting.

Hicksite Friends during this period were drifting towards an acceptance of some components of the larger American culture, and one example of this was the adoption of elements of mainstream ecclesiastical architecture. [clxiii] This was manifested at Plumstead by changing the location of the facing benches to the east gable, thereby making the west gable-end entry the main door and creating a more churchlike appearance.

A photo of the interior of the Plumstead Meetinghouse, looking towards the facing benches, with the rare iron stove *in situ*. The photo was taken in 1936, but the appearance in 1875 would have been much the same. Photo courtesy of Friends Historical Library

Retaining the south-facing doorway provided convenient access to the burying ground, and a view over the Pine Run valley. A new and rather elaborate iron stove of unusual design was purchased, which was destined, years later, to become part of Henry Mercer's museum collection.

Thaddeus Kenderdine reported that some new benches had been made, but mostly the old ones were still being used. [clxiv]

Plumstead's iron ten plate stove, shown in Mercer Museum storage. It was unusual in that it was never intended for cooking. The lower chamber was designed for a wood fire, and the barred upper chamber radiated heat into the room. Note the large cracks. Photo by Dafydd Jones

PLUMSTEAD MEETING AT THE TURN OF THE CENTURY

Attendance at Meeting for Worship seems to have been fairly regular during the next twenty years, as the minutes reported, "All of our meetings for worship and discipline have been attended except… for one at Plumstead, non-attendance was owing to inclement weather." [clxv]Plumstead also had its own treasurer and a buildings and grounds committee within Buckingham Meeting. [clxvi]A First Day School was started in 1876, and for a while it prospered, with attendance reaching one hundred. This number would have included children and adult members, plus nonmembers from the neighborhood.

In 1891, R. S. Haviland wrote about his visit to Plumstead Meeting in the *Friends Intelligencer and Journal*: "First Day morning dawned bright and cold. A ride of about five miles brought us to Plumstead Meetinghouse, which is pleasantly situated on a high hill, commanding an extended view over a beautiful country. This meeting was established in 1730, and the house was built in 1750. It is of stone and in a good state of preservation.

"The house was well filled and the meeting was to us an exceptionally pleasant one in the presence of so many children, who came with their parents and were very bright and attentive. They pressed forward to speak with the strangers after the meeting and gladdened our hearts with their childlike friendliness. About one quarter of the meeting were Mennonites, a plain and substantial people, whose kindly greetings expressed that they have much in common with our Society, in practical testimony and life, at least." [27]

The meetinghouse was also being used for purposes other than religious services, such as the lecture about Plumstead Township given in 1885 by historian W.W.H. Davis. In 1899, the PYM Philanthropic Committee held a conference at Plumstead Meetinghouse, with the keynote speaker addressing the subject of "Peace and Arbitration." [clxvii]

But once again, after the turn of the century and a generation later, Plumstead was declining. In 1903, the Monthly Meeting reported that at Plumstead "some Friends duly attend; but much loss is felt from the indifference and neglect of many others." [clxviii] There were fourteen Friends at Plumstead Indulged Meeting, [clxix] and in the six months prior to February, 1903, there were eight Sundays when no one at all attended Meeting for Worship.[clxx] The First Day School had been discontinued due to a "dearth of members" children and an ungrateful

27 Haviland, p. 186. He goes on to add… "A few things are noticeable in all the meetinghouses in this section: 1. they are capacious and evidently intended for large congregations; 2. they were honestly built, and built to last, being very solid structures of stone, with the evident expectancy that the Society of Friends had come to stay; and 3. the evident taste and refinement of those early Friends, evinced in the neat paneling of the shutters and trimming of the woodwork in the building. They must have been quite as tasteful as the dwellings of that early day."

neighborhood."[clxxi] The meetinghouse had not been repainted since the rebuilding in 1875, the fences were "dilapidated,"[clxxii] and the roof of one shed was "open to the sky."[clxxiii] However, this situation was soon to improve, since the Samuel Jeanes Fund eventually approved $150.00 for the repairs, and the interest from a $1,000.00 bequest was also available.[clxxiv]

The Plumstead Meetinghouse circa 1900. Courtesy of Friends Historical Library

Membership at Buckingham Monthly Meeting (which included the indulged meetings at Doylestown and Plumstead) was steadily declining during the nineteenth and early twentieth centuries, and it dropped below two hundred members for the first time in 1917.[28] The Spanish influenza epidemic the following year caused

[28] It was estimated to have been over 1,000 members c. 1800 (Kirson, 1923)

further problems, as recorded in the minutes: "Owing to the prevalence of epidemic influenza all meetings, churches, schools, etc. were closed by order of the State Commission of Health on 10th month 5th day and were not again opened until 11th month 3rd day, consequently no meetings were held in any of our meeting houses for either worship or discipline during that time." [clxxv]In general, however, regular weekly meetings for worship were being held at Plumstead, with a few exceptions, through 1927, the last year that information was recorded in the minutes. A visitor in 1929 reported that Plumstead Meeting was irregularly kept up by the few members of the Society located in the neighborhood, but that the meetinghouse was in good repair and a caretaker was engaged to look after it. [clxxvi]

At Buckingham Monthly Meeting of Friends held at Doylestown Ninth Mo 2nd 1918

Owing to the prevalence of Epidemic Influenza all meetings churches, Schools &c, were closed by order of the State Commission of health on 10 mo. 5. and were not again opened untill 11th mo. 3. consequently no meetings were held in any of our meeting houses for either worship or discipline during that time.

Over the next decade, Buckingham's Plumstead Buildings and Grounds Committee was able to afford necessary repairs through the interest on funds held in trust, and supplemented as needed in various ways, such as the sale of sheds, rental from the tenant house, and grant money from the Samuel Jeanes Fund. [clxxvii] In 1939, the committee reported that all necessary repairs had been made to the Plumstead

Meetinghouse, and all outside woodwork had been given two coats of paint. The caretaker's house and the gates to the graveyard had been painted as well, and the fence along the highway had been white-washed. [clxxviii] Plumstead's funds were kept separate from those of Buckingham, and during the Great Depression, its financial security was impressive. In 1933, Buckingham Monthly Meeting needed to take money out of the preparative meeting's savings, and borrow from Plumstead's funds to meet its Quarterly Meeting quota. Despite attempting other measures to improve the situation, in 1939, Buckingham found itself unable to meet the quota at all. [clxxix]Doylestown, in the meantime "finding itself seriously affected by lack of funds" needed to ask the Quarterly Meeting to pay its fire tax. [clxxx]

A DECLINE IS FOLLOWED BY GRADUAL REAWAKENING

In 1941, Helen Williams and Rachel DuBois of Buckingham Meeting arranged affairs for a weekly Meeting for Worship at Plumstead from May through September. This was repeated in the following two years. Meetings for Worship in warm weather declined sporadically over the next decade to one annual meeting in September by the early 1950s.

Without a regular congregation to supply financial support, upkeep of the buildings and grounds now became an ever increasing problem.

Plumstead Meeting's income from the trust funds had not kept pace with inflation, and a "lack of funds" prevented a list of needed repairs to the buildings from getting done. Two of the "drive sheds" were torn down in 1950. The graveyard walls were badly in need of repair and a list of graves in the graveyard was needed. [clxxxi] In addition, the deeds and other Plumstead records were in disarray. In 1953, the Plumstead Building and Grounds Committee began to address the situation. A survey was conducted of the Plumstead property, and a new deed transferred it to the incorporated Trustees of Buckingham Friends Meeting.

Courtesy of Friends Historical Library

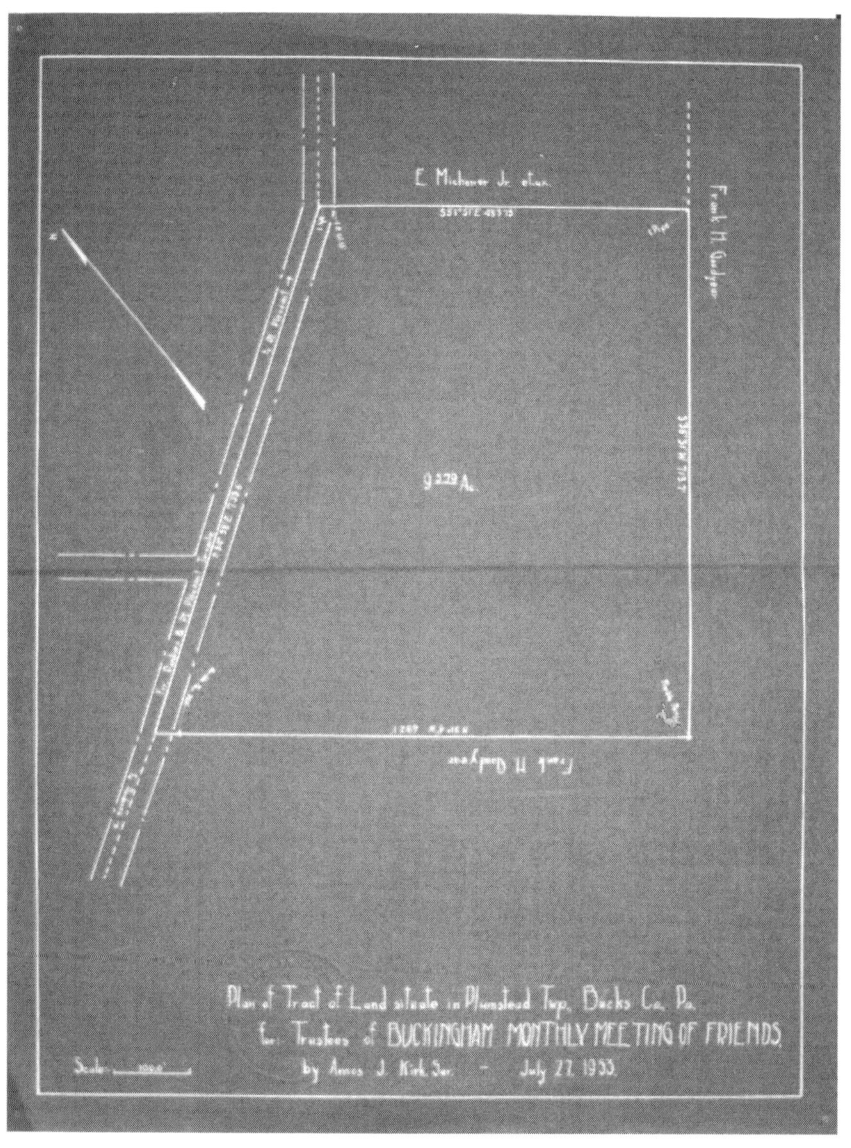
E. Michener Jr. et ux.
Frank H. Gallagher
Plan of Tract of Land situate in Plumstead Twp., Bucks Co., Pa.
for Trustees of BUCKINGHAM MONTHLY MEETING OF FRIENDS
by Amos J. Kirk, Sur. - July 27, 1933.

Laura Fell painstakingly combed through all the old Buckingham minutes and created a booklet about the history of Plumstead Friends Meeting in time for its 225th anniversary. Comly Michener, whose family had many members interred in the Plumstead burial ground, began identifying the grave sites. By 1965, he had compiled a fifteen-page booklet of the history of the burial ground which also contained an index to hundreds of graves.

A crisis developed in 1956 upon the death of the property caretaker, who had been living in the tenant house for many years. A new tenant was needed to help cover the ongoing expenses with insurance, property taxes, and lawn mowing, but the house additionally needed repairs and improvements to make it more habitable. One proposed solution was to sell the house and the taxable land around it. Instead, by selling a portion of vacant land along the west side of the property totaling about four-and-a-half acres, there was enough money to retain and fix the house, and also do the most urgent repairs on the meetinghouse while reducing future property taxes.

The house was kept as a source of revenue, and the hope was that the rent from a new tenant would finance the repairs needed to restore 500 feet of the graveyard wall. [29]When another four years passed with the graveyard walls still in a state of disrepair, the Michener family donated $1,000.00 toward the $1,165.00 expense. [clxxxii]

---

[29] Buckingham Monthly Meeting minutes, 3rd mo./3rd d./1956. Minutes from August 1956 indicate that of the $4597 raised from the sale, $3400 was spent repairing the tenant house.

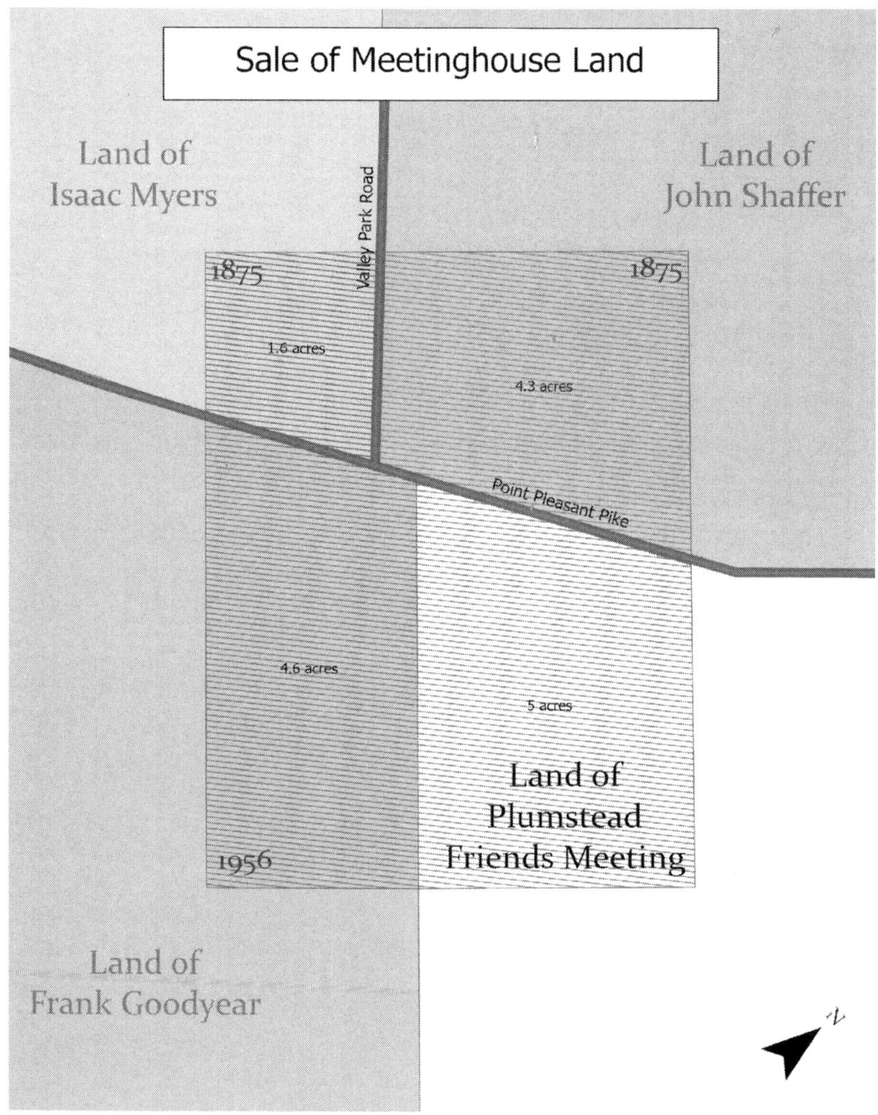

A map showing the reduction of Plumstead Meeting land from the original 15 acres to a current parcel of just under 5 acres. Map by Whitley Gray

Over the years, there were Doan family gatherings and Michener reunions at Plumstead, and an annual Meeting for Worship that increased to twice a year in the 1960s. In 1966, Sadie Taylor, a First Day School teacher at Doylestown Meeting, and her class of teenagers wanted to do something special for Christmas Eve. They arranged to have a Christmas Carol sing at the Plumstead Meetinghouse, and the event was so popular that it became an annual tradition.

Photo by Dafydd Jones

In the years that followed, Maris Langford often invited the entire Doylestown Meeting to her home on Christmas Eve following the candlelight service at Plumstead. [clxxxiii]Friends from Doylestown began holding Meeting for Worship at the Plumstead Meetinghouse every August, and occasional weddings were held there under Doylestown's care.

In 1988, Sadie's sister, Beth Taylor, felt led to reopen Plumstead Meeting on a regular basis; Doylestown and Buckingham Meetings were both supportive. Permission was granted by Bucks Quarterly Meeting, and thus the Plumstead Worship Group was formed. There were originally about fifteen attenders, and regular business meetings were held with Beth Taylor acting as clerk. The worship group made financial contributions to BQM and PYM, and they shared the cost of upkeep of the meetinghouse and grounds with Buckingham. [clxxxiv]Quarterly reports were made to the Plumstead Committee of Buckingham Monthly Meeting. There was a lively First Day School group that met on the porch, then for a while in the old outhouse, and, after 1998, in the sunroom of the tenant house. Christmas Eve candlelight singing and an Easter egg hunt in the burial ground were events to which the entire neighborhood was invited.

PLUMSTEAD MONTHLY MEETING FORMS

Each year, the question as to whether the Worship Group wished to become a Monthly Meeting was raised, and each year the answer was no, until 2001. At the September 2001 Meeting for Business, "a discussion was held about the possibility of becoming a monthly meeting, with many different thoughts being shared. It appeared that most of us wanted Plumstead to remain the same, while Carol Ann Gray reflected that she thought of it as a commitment." [30]

---

30 Plumstead Worship Group minutes, September 16, 2001. My reflection was, in fact, a response to a comment that words do not matter, and that the gatherings at Plumstead would be what they were whether they were called the Plumstead Worship Group or Plumstead Monthly Meeting. I disagreed, saying that if we became a monthly meeting, the attenders who were not Quakers would have the opportunity to join the Society of Friends with a membership resting at Plumstead. This would become part of their identity, and they could think of themselves and call themselves Quakers. Those of us who were already Quakers could transfer our memberships from other meetings to Plumstead, and end our fragmentation of energy and

After that meeting, there was a willingness to investigate further, although many concerns were expressed, particularly in regard to Plumstead's responsibilities towards Bucks Quarter. By November, a consensus had been reached for Plumstead to apply to Buckingham Monthly Meeting and then to Bucks Quarter to become a Monthly Meeting. There were two threshing sessions with Buckingham, after which it was agreed that Plumstead would be entirely responsible for the maintenance of the meetinghouse and the lawn around it (plus an annual mowing of the field behind the tenant house). The deed for the property would remain with Buckingham, but members of Plumstead were free to do as they wished with the meetinghouse and grounds as long as Buckingham was kept informed. An application to become a monthly meeting was then made to the clerk of Bucks Quarterly Meeting. By May 2002, the application had been approved and sent to Philadelphia Yearly Meeting, [clxxxv] which responded with "joy in having Plumstead Friends Meeting join our spiritual fellowship in Philadelphia Yearly Meeting. Your witness to the Light in coming together to worship and work as a new Friends Meeting strengthens all of us in our spiritual journeys." [clxxxvi]

The first meeting for business as Plumstead Monthly Meeting was held in June 2002. It was decided that anyone who had been part of the Worship Group would automatically become a member of the new meeting after making a written request. Bob Happ wrote: "I wish to join Plumstead Friends Meeting" and became its first member.

---

resources. All of these things, and a public declaration to be a monthly meeting community, might well create a positive change. Words do make a difference, I said. For example, imagine that a couple with a long standing relationship had a wedding, made a public declaration of commitment, and returned later that day to the home they had left that morning. But because of those words that were said that day, something had changed within them, and how society would treat them.

137 Callowhill Road
Chalfont, PA 18914

Dear Friends:

I would like to join Plumstead Friends Meeting of the Religious Society of Friends.

Sincerely,

Robert J. Happ

Robert J. Happ

A total of twenty-eight people joined Plumstead Monthly Meeting during that initial year.

In the subsequent years, many improvements were made to the interior of the meetinghouse, including repainting the walls and buying new rugs and bench cushions. The porch was enclosed with thermal glass, a more efficient stove was purchased, and the meetinghouse floor was replaced. Plumbing and electricity were not added, however, thus maintaining the colonial character of the building, and providing a very "green" conservation of natural resources. Improvements on the grounds included rebuilding the carriage shed (after it had been demolished by a car), and the purchase of a 10x12 foot frame structure, heated with a propane space heater, which became a dedicated First Day School space.

Today, Plumstead remains an active community, acting as a beneficial presence in a variety of ways. Among these are the donation of money, food, clothing and supplies to local, regional, and international relief organizations. In 2008, in conjunction with Lutheran Family Services and a number of other Quaker meetings, Plumstead Meeting provided critical support to an Iraqi family resettling in the area.

Photo used with permission of Issam Alazawee

In 2012, a scene in the movie *The North Star*, a story of the journey of two escaped slaves, was filmed in the Plumstead Meetinghouse. The grounds of Plumstead Meeting became a temporary memorial in 2018, with a display of fifty colored T-shirts on the lawn. Each shirt bore the name of a Bucks County victim of gun violence, calling attention to the impact of such violence here and beyond.

Photo by Harry Branson

Plumstead Friends Meeting is now in its twentieth year as a monthly meeting, and is approaching its three hundredth year since the first Meetings for Worship were held at the home of Thomas Brown. Throughout its long history, Plumstead Quakers overcame the adverse circumstances of pioneer days, and persecution during the Revolutionary War. They endured bitter division within the Society, and then, optimistic about their future, rebuilt the entire meetinghouse. After a period of relative inactivity, Quakers returned a few decades later to enjoy once again the quiet and simplicity of a country meetinghouse. This is a story of one Meeting's resilience and spiritual journey, trusting (in the words of George Fox) in the Ocean of Light. Plumstead has now emerged from a worldwide pandemic with a sense that whatever unexpected things the future brings, Friends remain open to the leadings of that Light.

VIGNETTE:

THE SCHOOL AND BURYING GROUND AT PLUMSTEAD MEETING

PLUMSTEAD FRIENDS SCHOOL

In colonial America, education was available only to the privileged few who could afford to pay for private instruction. Although Quakers downplayed education as intellectualism that detracted from spiritual experience, they did provide their children with the fundamentals that would enable work and reading of the Bible. Towards the end of the eighteenth century, a special effort was made by Philadelphia Yearly Meeting to see that every Monthly Meeting supported a Friends elementary school. [31]

[31] In 1777, Yearly Meeting recommended that a lot of ground be provided in each Monthly or Preparative Meeting, sufficient for a garden, orchard, etc., and that a suitable dwelling, stable, etc., be erected thereon. And that funds be raised by contributions bequests, etc., in each Meeting; the interest of which to be applied either in aid of the tutor's salary or lessening the expense of Friends in straitened circumstances in the education of their children. And that a committee be appointed in each meeting to have the case of schools and the funds for their support and that no tutor be employed but with their consent. (Wickersham, 1886, p. 85) See also Buckingham Monthly Meeting minutes, 4th d/12th mo./1780, which reported PYM's encouraging monthly and quarterly meetings to continue their attention to the establishment of schools.

In Plumstead, the early minutes reflect that a school had already been established on the land that Thomas Brown donated to establish Plumstead Meeting in 1730. Several references, however, regard 1752 as the date that an official school was established at Plumstead. The most specific of these says, "In 1752, the log [meetinghouse] was replaced by a two story high native gray stone structure. A smaller building, one story high and constructed of the same material, was attached to the end of the meetinghouse at the same time for use as a school." [clxxxvii] The Buckingham Monthly minutes do not give details as to their individual schools, but one source indicates that the Plumstead school was kept open a part of each year from 1752 until 1816, except for 1777, when the meetinghouse was used as a hospital.[clxxxviii]

Quaker schools were pioneers in at least three fields: the equal education of boys and girls, the use of nonviolent methods, and the introduction of scientific and practical subjects into the curriculum. It was natural that a religious body whose faith was based on experience should relate education to that which can be experienced. The school community, through its meetings for worship, its daily readings from the Bible, and by the influence of religiously minded and dedicated teachers also created a setting in which religious feelings developed. [clxxxix]

The minutes for 2nd d./8th mo./1790 give the following report: "It appears that Preparatory to the Plan printed out by Yearly Meeting in 1778 and again recommended last year, there are two school houses under the Direction of [Buckingham] Meeting. Schools in general amongst us, both as to tutors and school government are in a better state than they formerly were. And some property hath been vested in the Meeting towards a fund for the use of schools. Nineteen sets at Buckingham and one at Plumstead of Gough's *History of the People Called Quakers* subscribed for." [cxc]

Attention being given to the General Accounts of Care exersised in most Places for the Promotion of well regulated Schools for the Instruction of the Youth in Usefull Learning there appears a Ground of hope that this Momentious Concern is gradually making Way in the minds of Friends and a desier prevailing that our Brethern every where may be encouraged to percevere in this desirable Work a continued close Regard to its Importance and the evil Consequences resulting from a neglect of it is earnestly urged afresh to the vigilent Care of Friends in each Quarter to be extended not only to the Children of Friends of more easy Circumstances in life but also to the Offspring of those that are Poor and of the Black People whose Condition give them a Claim to that Benefit consistent with the Sence of this Meeting contained in the repeated Advises given forth The Quarterly Meetings to send Accounts to the Meeting next Year of the further Progress made in this good Work

A

HISTORY

OF THE

PEOPLE CALLED QUAKERS.

From their firſt Riſe to the preſent Time.

Compiled from AUTHENTIC RECORDS, and from the WRITINGS of that PEOPLE.

By JOHN GOUGH.

IN FOUR VOLUMES.

VOL. IV.

DUBLIN:

PRINTED BY ROBERT JACKSON, MEATH-STREET.

M.DCC.XC.

Gough's History of the People Called Quakers appeared in four volumes in 1790. This volume is owned by Plumstead Meeting.

The most prominent Plumstead student of that era was Charles Huston, (1771–1849), who later became a Pennsylvania supreme court justice. Davis reports that the Huston family, although not Quaker, sent Charles "to school in the old meetinghouse, his father at the time keeping the tavern at Gardenville." [cxci]

By 1807, there were five schools within Buckingham Monthly Meeting, three "being kept" by members, with the other two being vacant. Funds were "amply sufficient for the schooling of poor children and also for the greater schooling of the children of Friends in straightened circumstances." [cxcii] From this point, however, at the same time that the membership of Friends was decreasing, the Friends schools also went into a consistent decline. The Buckingham Committee for the Oversight of Schools reported in 1820 that "the present situation of schools within the limits of this meeting is in a very deplorable and depressed state, in measure owing, we conceive, to the lack of pecuniary aid, and as there is a considerable sum of money belonging to this meeting, the interest whereof is unappropriated, and the necessity of the times are such, that the committee would suggest the propriety of using a part thereof by way of salary for the encouragement of a well-qualified tutor, embarking in that very important concern of society as the most practicable means of placing our schools in a more desirable situation." [cxciii]

A report by the committee on education in 1834 listed six reasons for the continued decline in Friends schools. [cxciv]

In addition to the identified problems, a particularly thorny issue during the schism was that there were two bodies who called themselves Buckingham Monthly Meeting laying claim to the same funds that had been given by bequest for the purpose of education.

26

1st. A want of properly appreciating the advantages of literary instruction in accordance with our religious principles & testimonies, may be ranked among the most prominent.

2nd. The establishment of the Boarding School at Westown; which as it provided for the education of the children of the Wealthy, drew off their influence & aid in the support of Common Schools.—

3rd. The pay for teaching not keeping pace with the advanced compensation received for other services, — this we conceive is the prominent cause of the great difficulty experienced in procuring well qualified members as teachers.

4th. A Committee appointed by the Preparative Meeting to have the care & Superintendance of our School near the Meeting house, & several other Friends who reside within the immediate vicinity thereof, have almost wholy withdrawn their interest & support therefrom & send their children to a private school in the neighbourhood, which nevertheless is taught by our own members, & justly deserves the encouragement of Friends whose interests are not confined to schools established agreeably to the advice of the Yearly Meeting

5th. And recently from the division that has taken place in the Society, which not only from its absorbing & distracting influence, has drawn the attention from other objects but by the derangement produced in the application of our funds has in a particular manner affected Schools.

6th. Friends on account of their scattered situation have not been able to support a School by themselves, their children never having been a majority — often a small part —
hence houses built and owned by the meeting have been used for the common Schools of the neighbourhood — since as the Masters Salary was made up by quarterly charges for each Scholar, — Friends have conformed to the views of the employers, both in selecting teachers, & in the order of the Schools.—

John Wilson
Signed by order of the Committee Rachel Pickering

The Pennsylvania constitutions of 1776 and 1790 both called for the establishment of a public education system, which was finally accomplished in 1834. Freedom and democracy called for a well-informed and educated public that could understand political issues and make wise decisions at the polls. At first the new system was optional, but in 1854 the common school system became mandatory throughout the state. [cxcv]Both Hicksite and Orthodox Meetings looked with skepticism on the rise of a public or common school system in Pennsylvania, in spite of the fact that the reformer most responsible for its creation was the Quaker Roberts Vaux.[32]

With the advent in 1855 of the adoption of public schooling by local governments, Buckingham sold two of its lots intended for schools, and the Plumstead General Subscription Fund for education was dissolved. During the 1875 renovation of the Plumstead Meetinghouse, several reports indicate it was shortened in length. Considering that the current foundation was not altered, perhaps it was the schoolhouse addition that was removed, thus permanently ending the era of the Plumstead Friends School.

THE BURYING GROUND

The Quaker testimony of simplicity, which impacted all areas of life, also impacted burial practices. Friends traditionally did not mark graves at all much before the nineteenth century, wishing to avoid immodest

32 Frost, "Years of Crisis and Separation", pp. 88,89. Frost adds that many rural Friends' schools were more like district schools than Quaker institutions because they were supported by a combination of private and public funds. In the 1850s the Yearly Meeting appointed an education committee and received a series of detailed reports and recommendations. Of the over 2,500 children in the report, more than forty percent were in non-Quaker institutions. The education committee warned that the survival of a distinctive form of religion was jeopardized, and advocated a series of reforms including creating endowments for Friends scholarships and schools.

"distinction" and stating "it is altogether wrong and of evil tendency for to have any grave stones or any other sort of monument over or about the graves in any of the Friends burying grounds." cxcvi

It Being Layd Before this Meeting by ye Quarterly Meeting of Philadelphia how much they are grieved & disatisfyed wth Grave Stones & Monuments over or about ye Graves in Friends Burying Ground; this Meeting taking ye matter into their Consideration; do give it as their Sense & judgmt that it is altogather wrong & of Evill tendency for to have any grave Stones or any Sort of Monuments over or about their Graves in any of Friends burying Grounds; & further that those Monuments that are already in ye Burying Ground Either of Wood or Stone shall be taken away & no new put up; but to be as sparing as friends well Can for those who were not friends and put up before the burying Ground was Solely Confirmed to friends.

So in old Quaker graveyards there are often many more interments than appearances suggest, with the oldest section of the burial ground being an unmarked lawn. Friends also did not originally lay out family plots, instead burying each person in the order of their death. cxcvii Gravesites progressed over time from being completely unmarked, to being marked with a plain brown native field stone, to having initials carved in the field stone, to having engraved low marble headstones. There are examples of all of these in the Plumstead burial ground. Later on, family plots came into use as well.

The first Plumstead meetinghouse was located at a place on the Brown property that already had a school and a graveyard, presumably a Brown family burial ground. The earliest burial the author could document in the Plumstead burying ground was that of the miller, John Dyer, who died in February 1738. [cxcviii] The location of his grave is unknown.

John Dyer departed this Life on the 31 Day of ye 11 mo
in the afternoon & was buried ye 2d of ye 12 month
in Friends Burying Ground at Plumstead | 1737
Elisabeth Dyer his Widow departed this Life ye 29 of ye 1 Month
and was buried in Friends Burying Ground at Plumstead | 1755

The log cabin meetinghouse was built in the northwest section of the current graveyard. According to Comly Michener, when the stone meetinghouse was constructed in 1752, a graveyard wall enclosing about one acre was built out of stone from the same quarry. The log meetinghouse was then demolished, opening up additional burial sites. [cxcix]

When Levi and Abraham Doan were hanged in 1788, they were buried outside of the Plumstead burial ground, as their lifestyle of crime was incompatible with the Quaker peace testimony. The Doan legend is still told today, and their well-marked graves remain objects of much curiosity.

In keeping with the conformity of the Quietist period, Philadelphia Yearly Meeting advised, in 1792, that Friends "be religiously guarded" in inviting non-Friends to Quaker burials. They also had numerous guidelines to prevent "the introduction of improper interments" at meetinghouses." [cc] Buckingham Monthly Meeting created, in response, guidelines for themselves which were more relaxed than the Yearly Meeting advice, proposing "that all persons who are the descendants of Friends and not being members of any other religious society and others living among us of orderly lives united in religious sentiment with Friends may be admitted to our present burying grounds, at the discretion of a committee appointed to the care of the same. And as there may be some instances of members in our religious society whose husband or wife may belong to some other religious society, and minor children serving apprenticeships amongst us, the surviving relation of such requesting to bury in our graveyard may be admitted provided they conform to the order of Friends." [cci]

The headstone of Abraham Doan, placed sometime after 1935. The original native stone marker is visible on the left, between the more modern ones. Photo by Alan Gray

During the Schism, Plumstead divided into two congregations. Members of the Plumstead Orthodox Meeting on Landisville Road, which lasted from approximately 1827 to 1877, had the option of burial, under Hicksite supervision, at the Plumstead meetinghouse on Point Pleasant Pike. As discussed in Chapter 5, maintenance and security at the burial ground became a concern as Plumstead declined in membership in the subsequent decades.

The cost for interment in 1893 at Plumstead was three dollars for adults and $1.50 for children under 12 years of age,[ccii] reminding us of how often in times past parents experienced the loss of their sons and daughters. Thaddeus Kinderdine, after visiting Plumstead in 1902, remarked upon a double grave of two little brothers who drowned together.

At that time, a tool shed existed in the graveyard, containing "an old-fashioned bier, such as was in use before handles were placed on coffins, and leather straps which had lowered the bodies of the dead of Plumstead for generations." [cciii]

The subsequent one hundred years saw attendance at Plumstead Friends Meeting diminish and finally cease for several decades. Burials slowed accordingly during this period, and for a while the graveyard walls fell into disrepair. Comly Michener remarked in 1965 that of the 554 marked graves, 82 had native brown stones, but that there had been many more in prior times. [33] Today 44 native brown stone markers survive. The remaining graves are marked with marble headstones, most being modest and low in height in the manner of Friends. The burial ground contains 800 graves in total and remains active.

---

[33] Michener, Comly, p. 1. Note also the Bucks County Historical Society has transcripts of gravestones taken about 1915 from the Plumstead Burial Ground.

The double headstone of brothers Charles and James Meginnes, who drowned together. The headstone is unusually tall and elaborate for a Quaker burying ground. The fingers point to an inscription which reads: 'Of such are the kingdom of heaven'

APPENDIX

SELECTED ORIGINAL DOCUMENTS

- A page from the 1747 Buckingham Monthly Meeting minutes
- A 1751 Spanish real found at Plumstead Meetinghouse grounds
- The Opening Remarks of the Extracts of the 1795 Philadelphia Yearly Meeting minutes
- The Meeting for Sufferings "Quaker Doctrine" of 1823
- The April 1827 Yearly Meeting Address (Green Street)
- The August 1827 Bucks Quarterly Meeting minutes (Orthodox)
- The October 1827 Philadelphia Yearly Meeting Epistle (Hicksite)
- The list of members of Plumstead Friends Meeting in 1827 and their affiliations
- A page from the 1859 Bucks County tax record for Plumstead Township

- A census of the composition of Buckingham and Plumstead Meetings in 1862
- A list of members of Plumstead Friends Meeting at the time it was laid down in 1869
- Documents relating to the rebuilding of the Plumstead Meetinghouse in 1875

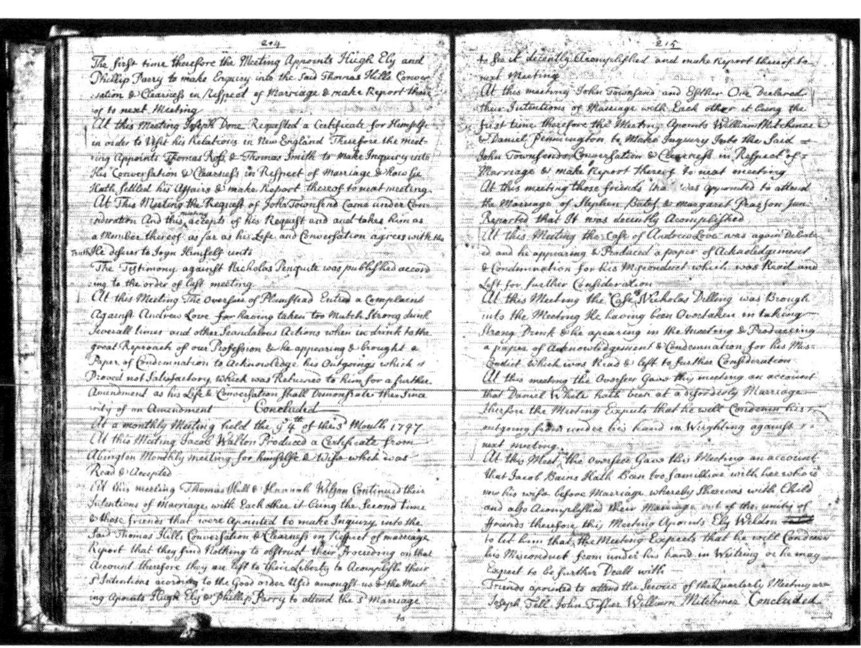

214

The first time therefore the Meeting Appoints Hugh Ely and
Phillip Parry to make Enquiry into the Said Thomas Hills Conversation & Clearness in Respect of Marriage & make Report thereof to next Meeting
At this Meeting Joseph Done Requested a Certificate for Himselfe
in order to Visit his Relations in New England Therefore the Meeting Appoints Thomas Ross & Thomas Smith to make Inquiry into
His Conversation & Clearness in Respect of Marriage & how he
Hath settled his Affairs & make Report thereof to next meeting.
At This Meeting the Request of John Townsend Came under Consideration And this meeting accepts of his Request and and takes him as
a Member thereof as far as his Life and Conversation agrees with the
truth He desires to Joyn Himselfe unto
The Testimony against Nicholas Penquite was published accord-
ing to the order of last meeting
At this Meeting The Overseers of Plumstead Entred a Complaint
Against Andrew Love for having taken too Mutch Strong drink
Severall times and other Scandalous Actions when in drink to the
great Reproach of our Profession & he appearing & brought a
Paper of Condemnation to Acknowledge his Outgoings which
Proved not Satisfactory which was Returned to him for a further
Amendment as his Life & Conversation shall Demonstrate the Since-
rity of an Amendment Concluded
At a monthly Meeting held the 9th 4th of the 3d Month 1797
At this Meeting Jacob Walton Produced a Certificate from
Abington Monthly meeting for himselfe & Wife which was
Read & Accepted
At this meeting Thomas Hill & Hannah Wilson Continued their
Intentions of Marriage with Each other it Being the Second time
& those friends that were Apointed to make Inquiry into the
Said Thomas Hills Conversation & Clearness in Respect of marriage
Report that they find Nothing to obstruct their Proceeding on that
Account therefore they are left to their Liberty to Accomplish their
Sd Intentions according to the Good order Used amongst us & the Meet-
ing Apoints Hugh Ely & Phillip Parry to attend the Sd Marriage
to

215

to See it decently Accomplished and make Report thereof to
next Meeting
At this meeting John Townsend and Esther Orr Declared
their Intentions of Marriage with Each other it being the
first time therefore the Meeting Apoints William Mitchener
& Daniel Pennington to Make Inquiry Into the Said
John Townsends Conversation & Clearness in Respect of
Marriage & make Report thereof to next meeting
At this meeting those friends that was appointed to attend
the Marriage of Stephen Bates & Margaret Pearson Jun
Reported that It was decently Accomplished
At this Meeting the Case of Andrew Love was again Debat-
ed and he appearing & Produced a paper of Acknowledgement
& Condemnation for his Misconduct which was Read and
Left for further Consideration
At this Meeting the Case of Nicholas Dilling was Brought
into the Meeting He having been Overtaken in taking
Strong Drink & he appearing in the Meeting & Produceing
a paper of Acknowledgement & Condemnation for his Misconduct Which was Read & left to further Consideration
At this meeting the Overseer Gave this meeting an account
that Daniel White hath been at a disorderly Marriage
therefore the Meeting Expects that he will Condemn his
outgoing from under his hand in Wrighting against
next meeting
At this Meeting the Overseer Gave this Meeting an account
that Jacob Baines Hath Been too familliar with her who is
now his wife before Marriage whereby She was with Child
and also Accomplished their Marriage out of the unity of
ffriends therefore this Meeting Apoints Ely Weldon
to let him that the Meeting Expects that he will Condemn
his Misconduct from under his hand in Writing or he may
Expect to be further Dealt with
Friends apointed to attend the Service of the Quarterly Meeting are
Joseph Fell John Fisher William Mitchener Concluded

This Spanish (Mexican) silver real, dated 1751, was found on the grounds of the Plumstead Meetinghouse. It was a common currency during colonial times. Photo by Dafydd Jones.

143

Meeting were produced & read. The weighty Matters therein contained, are recommended to the close Attention of all our Members. The Extracts are as follows, to wit,

Extracts from the Minutes of our Yearly Meeting for Pennsylvania, New-Jersey, Delaware & the Eastern Parts of Maryland & Virginia, held in Philadelphia, by Adjournments, from the 28th of the 9th Month to the 3d of the 10th Month inclusive 1795

29th of the Month, & 3d of the Week. The printed general Epistle, from the last Yearly Meeting of our Brethren in London, being read; and the weighty Contents, obtaining close Attention; 4000 Copies of an Abstract thereof, are directed to be printed for general Use

1st of the 10mo & 5th of the Week. On renewed Attention to the State of the Church as set forth in the Summary of the Reports from the Quarters, a lively Sence of the prevailing influence of a Worldly Spirit, as the radical Cause of Defection, occasioning sorrowful Complaints in various Instances, being witnessed to impress & animate the Minds of divers Brethren; producing the Communication of Weighty Observation & Edifying Counsel, wherein was traced with clearness & pertinence, both the secret Operation & open Effects of that Spirit; so debilitating & obstructive to religious Progress; not only evident, in a Conformity, to vain Modes & Customs in Dress, Address, Sumptuous Buil-

dings

144

dings & Furniture, with the Pomp & Ostentation observable, not unfrequently, at Marriages; — but peculiarly in those continued Causes of deep Exercise, the neglect of attending religious Meetings, and the ~~drowsy~~ sleepy Disposition acknowledged in Some who do attend.

The promoting a free Use of distilled Spirits, by distilling importing or vending of them as a Commodity in Trade, also, on a revival of the Subject, exiting a Degree of fervent Zeal, under the Influence whereof, the Ruin & Desolation proceeding from an intemperate Use of this inflamatory Article, both in Individuals & Nations, was affectingly set forth. And the Minute of this Meeting thereon of last Year being recurred to, its purport is afresh recommended to Quarterly & Monthly Meetings; which are exhorted to a continued exercise of faithful Labour, in patient Stability, guarding against Discouragement, which, given way to, will disqualify for this necessary Service, — Of the Effect whereof, they are desired to give account next Year.

Same Day, Afternoon, — The faithful Maintenance of our Christian Testimony against the Spirit of War & Contention, and the taking or administering of Oaths, engaging & exercising Friends, under an Earnest Concern that the solid gospel Ground of these Testimonies may be so uprightly attended to, as to be fully & clearly understood, and the Benefit resulting from a faithful adherence thereto, be rendered by our practice more extensively manifested in the World

and

2

At a Meeting for Sufferings held in Philadelphia the 17th of the 1st month 1823.

An Essay containing a few brief extracts from the writings of our primitive friends on several of the doctrines of the Christian religion, which have been always held and are most surely believed by us, being produced and read; on solid consideration, they appeared so likely to be productive of benefit if a publication thereof was made and spread among our members generally, that the Committee appointed on the printing and distribution of religious books, are directed to have a sufficient number of them struck off and distributed accordingly. — being as follows.

We have always believed that the Holy Scriptures were written by Divine inspiration, that they are able to make wise unto salvation thro' faith which is in Christ Jesus: for, as holy men of God spake as they were moved by the Holy Ghost, they are therefore profitable for doctrine, for reproof, for correction, for instruction in righteousness, that the man of God may be perfect thoroughly furnished unto all good works. — But they are not or cannot be subjected to the fallen, corrupt reason of man. — We have always asserted our willingness, that all our doctrines be tried by them; and admit it as a positive maxim, That whatsoever any do (pretending to the Spirit) which is contrary to the Scriptures, be accounted and judged a delusion of the devil. ——

We receive and believe in the testimony of the Scriptures simply as it stands in the Text — "There are three that bear record in heaven, the Father, the "Word, and the Holy Ghost, and these three are one." —— We believe in the only wise, omnipotent and everlasting God, the Creator of all things in heaven and earth, and the preserver of all that he hath made, who is God over all blessed for ever. —— The infinite and most wise God, who is the foundation, root and spring of all operation, hath wrought all things by his eternal Word and Son. This is that Word that was in the beginning with God, and was God, by whom all things were made, and without whom was not any thing made that was made. — Jesus Christ is the beloved and only begotten Son of God, who in the fulness of time, thro the Holy Ghost, was conceived and born of the virgin Mary: in him we have redemption thro his blood, even the forgiveness of sins. —— We believe that he was made a sacrifice for sin, who knew no sin; that he was crucified for us in the flesh, was buried and rose again the third day, by the power of his Father, for our justification, ascended up into heaven, and now sitteth at the right hand of God. ——

As then that infinite and incomprehensible Fountain of life and motion, operateth in the Creatures by his own eternal Word and power, so no creature has access again unto him but in and by the Son, according to his own blessed declaration, "No man knoweth the Father but the Son, and he to whom the Son will "reveal him," again, "I am the way, the Truth and the life: no man cometh "unto the Father but by me." — Hence he is the only Mediator between God and man: for having been with God from all eternity, being himself God, and also in time partaking of the nature of man, thro him is the goodness and love of God conveyed to mankind; and by him again man receiveth and partaketh of these mercies.

We acknowledge that of ourselves we are not able to do any thing that is good; neither can we procure remission of sins or justification by any act of our own; but acknowledge all to be <u>of</u> and <u>from</u> his love, which is the original and fundamental cause of our acceptance.– "For God so loved the world, that he "gave his only begotten Son, that whosoever believeth in him, should not "perish, but have everlasting life."

We firmly believe, it was necessary that Christ should come, that by his death and sufferings, he might offer up himself a sacrifice to God for our sins, who his own self bare our sins in his own body on the tree; so we believe that the remission of sins which any partake of, is only in and by virtue of that most satisfactory sacrifice, and no otherwise. For it is by the obedience of that One, that the free gift is come upon all to justification. — Thus Christ by his death and sufferings, hath reconciled us to God even while we are enemies; that is, he offers reconciliation to us; and we are thereby put into a capacity of being reconciled. God is willing to be reconciled unto us and ready to remitt the sins that are past, if we repent.

Jesus Christ is the intercessor and advocate with the Father in heaven, appearing in the presence of God for us, being touched with a feeling of our infirmities, sufferings and sorrows; and also by his spirit in our hearts, he maketh intercession according to the will of God, crying abba Father. He tasted death for every man, shed his blood for all men, and is the propitiation for our sins, and not for ours only, but also for the sins of the whole world. He alone is our Redeemer and Saviour, the captain of our salvation, the promised Seed who bruises the serpent's head, the Alpha and Omega, the first and the last. He is our wisdom, righteousness, justification and redemption; neither is there salvation in any other; for there is no other name under heaven given among men, whereby we may be saved.

As he ascended far above all heavens, that he might fill all things; his fulness cannot be comprehended, or contained in any finite creature, but in some measure known and experienced in us, as we are prepared to receive the same; as of his fulness we have received, grace for grace. — He is both the word of faith and a quickening Spirit in us, whereby he is the immediate cause, author, object and strength of our living faith in his name and power, and of the work of our salvation from sin and bondage of corruption. The Son of God cannot be divided from the least or lowest appearance of his own divine Light or Life in us, no more than the Sun from its own light: Nor is the sufficiency of his Light within, set up or mentioned in opposition to him, or to his fulness considered as in himself or without us: Nor can any measure or degree of light received from Christ, be properly called the fulness of Christ, or Christ as in fulness, nor exclude him from being our complete Saviour.– And where the least degree or measure of this Light and life of Christ within, is sincerely waited in, followed and obeyed, there is a blessed increase of light and Grace known and felt; as the path of the Just it shines more and more until the perfect day, and thereby a growing in grace, and in the knowledge of God, and of our Lord and Saviour Jesus Christ, hath been and is truly experienced.

Wherefore we say, that whatever Christ then did both living and dying, was of great benefit to the salvation of all that have believed, and now do, and that hereafter shall believe in him unto justification and acceptance with God: but

but the way to come to that faith, is, to receive and obey the manifestation of his divine Light and grace in the conscience, which leads men to believe and value, and not to disown or undervalue Christ as the common sacrifice and Mediator. For we do affirm, that to follow this holy Light in the conscience, and to turn our minds, and bring all our deeds and thoughts to it, is the readiest, nay the only right way, to have true, living and sanctifying faith in Christ, as he appeared in the flesh; and to discern the Lord's body, coming and sufferings aright, and to receive any real benefit by him as our only sacrifice and Mediator; according to the beloved disciple's emphatical testimony, "If we walk in the light as he (God) is in the light, we have fellowship one with another, and the blood of Jesus Christ his Son, cleanseth us from all sin." —

By the propitiatory sacrifice of Christ without us, we, truly repenting and believing, are thro' the mercy of God, justified from the imputation of sins and transgressions that are past, as tho' they had never been committed: And by the mighty work of Christ within us, the power, nature and habits of sin are destroyed; that as sin once reigned unto death, even so now Grace reigneth thro' righteousness unto eternal life, by Jesus Christ our Lord. —

Signed on behalf of
the Meeting

Jonan. Evans — clerk

A printed address of Friends within the compass of the Yearly Meeting held in Philadelphia issued by a large number of friends from the different branches of the said Yearly Meeting convened at Green Street meetinghouse and held by adjournments from the 19th of the 4th month 1827 to the 21st of the same inclusive which being read after deliberate and solid consideration it is concluded to recommend it with our reports to the attention of the ensuing Quarterly Meeting. The address being as follows:

AN ADDRESS to FRIENDS within the compass of the Yearly Meeting held in Philadelphia:

At a meeting of a large number of friends from the different branches of the Yearly Meeting held in Philadelphia, convened at Green Street meetinghouse, on the 19th of the 4th month 1827, to confer together on the present unsettled state of the SOCIETY OF FRIENDS and to consider what measures it may be proper to take in the openings of Truth, to remedy the distressing evil: after a solemn pause, and under a deep sense of the weighty subject it was unitedly concluded to address the members of this Yearly Meeting on the affecting occasion; for which purpose an essay being produced, and some progress made in the consideration thereof, the meeting adjourned; to meet again by Divine permission tomorrow evening.

4th month,20th Friends again met and resumed the consideration of the aforesaid Address, which after deliberate attention, was with some alterations, unanimously adopted, when the meeting adjourned, to meet again tomorrow.

4th month, 21st Friends assembled, pursuant to adjournment. The essay of an Address being again read, and weightily considered, it was agreed that it be signed on behalf of this meeting, and that a suitable number of copies be printed for distribution.

TO FRIENDS within the compass of the Yearly Meeting held in Philadelphia

DEAR FRIENDS,

The members of the Society of Friends have been permitted, in time past, to be partakers together under the Divine blessing, of the excellent effects produced by the power of that Gospel which was professed and lived in by the Apostles, and which, after a long night of apostacy, was embraced by our worthy ancestors. We are prepared to record our full conviction, that this same Gospel continues to be open to us and to all men, and is "the power of God unto salvation" to those that believe in and obey it. Its blessed fruits are love to God and love to man, manifested in life and conduct: and our early Friends gave ample proof of the tendency and influence of the "new commandment" which Christ gave to his Disciples when he said "A new commandment I give unto you, that ye love one another: as I have loved you, that ye also love one another." Through an obedience to it, they became known and distinguished: acting under its sacred influence and government, they were made powerful instruments in opening the door of gospel liberty, and removing many of the fetters that had been formed in the dark night of superstition and error that preceded them. Hence they were prepared to promulgate to the glorious truth, that God alone is the Sovereign Lord of Conscience, and that with this unalienable right, no power, civil or ecclesiastical, should ever interfere. This blessed liberty was amply enjoyed among themselves, and through faithfulness- not to speculative opinions, but kept to the light of Christ within- They were thus united in the one eternal, unchangeable spirit, and by it became of one heart and one mind. In this truly Christian state, they were light in the world, and as a city set on an hill which cannot be hid. Through their instrumentality, with the blessing of the Almighty upon their labours, our religious Society became professed of this very important spiritual inheritance and we feel bound to endeavor to preserve it, unfettered by the hand of man, and unalloyed with prescribed modes of faith, framed in the will and wisdom of the creature.

With this great object in view, our attention has been turned to the present condition of this Yearly Meeting and its different branches; and by evidence on every hand, we are constrained to declare, that the unity of this body is interrupted- that a division exists among us developing in its progress views which appear incompatible with each other, and feelings averse to reconciliation. Doctrines held by one part of Society and which we believe, to be sound and edifying, are pronounced by the other part to be unsound and spurious. From this has resulted a state of things that has proved destructive of peace and tranquility, and in which the fruits of love and condescension have been blasted, and the comforts and enjoyments even of social intercourse greatly diminished. Measures have been pursued which we deem oppressive, and in their nature and their tendency calculated to undermine and destroy those benefits to establish and perpetuate which should be the purpose of every religious association.

It is only under the influence of the peaceable spirit and wisdom of Jesus "that discipline can be properly administered, or the affairs of the Church transacted" with decency and in order. This blessed influence is a wall of defense, on the right hand and on the left, protecting all, even the weakest of the flock, and within this sacred enclosure our rights and privileges repose, as in the bosom of society, in perfect security. On this foundation has rested that excellent order which the Society of Friends has been favoured, in good degree, to maintain in its transactions; this is the bond that has united its Members together and enabled them to manage all their concerns in "forebearance and love of each other." But this blessed order has been infringed, both in the present Yearly Meeting, (producing inexampled disorder in some of its sittings), and in many of its subordinate branches, and has proved a fruitful source of the difficulties that now exist.

It is under a solemn and deliberate view of this painful state of our affairs, that we feel bound to express to you, under a settled conviction of mind that the period has fully come in which we ought to look toward making a quiet retreat from this scene of confusion and we therefore recommend ti you deeply to weigh this momentous subject and to adopt such a course as Truth, under solid and solemn deliberation, may point to, in furtherance of this object, that our Society may again enjoy the free exercise of its right and privileges . And we think it proper to remind you that we have no new Gospel to preach; nor any other foundation to lay than that already laid and proclaimed by our forefathers, even "Christ within, the hope of Glory-the power of God, and the wisdom of God." Neither have we any other system of Discipline to propose, than that which we already profess, believing that, whilst we sincerely endeavor to walk consistently with our holy profession, and to administer it in the spirit of forebearance and love, it will be found sufficient for the government of the Church. And whilst we cherish a reasonable hope to see our Zion, under the Divine blessing, loosen herself from the bands of her neck and put on her strength, and Jerusalem her "beautiful garments", and our Annual and other assemblies again crowned with that quietude and peace which become our Christian profession; we feel an ardent desire that in all our proceedings tending to this end, our conduct toward our brethren may, on every occasion, be marked with love and forebearance: that when reviled, we bless, when defamed, we entreat; and when persecuted, that we suffer it.

Finally, brethren, we beseech you "by the name of our Lord, Jesus Christ, that ye speak the same thing, and there be no divisions among you; but that ye be perfectly joined together, in the same mind, and in the same judgement." And now we commend you to God, and to the Word of his Grace, which is able to build you up, and to give you an inheritance among all them which are sanctified."

Signed by John Comly and 9 others.

This printed address is an explanation of why some Friends withdrew from Philadelphia Yearly Meeting in April, 1827, and met at Green Street. It was the opening salvo of the schism.

(1)

1827. 8 mo. At Bucks Quarterly Meeting of Friends held at the Falls, the thirteenth of the eighth month eighteen hundred and twentyseven.

A large number of our members with the Clerk seceded from our Yearly Meeting, and in addition to divers other acts violating the established order of our Discipline, read an address from a number of persons who express an intention of establishing a Yearly Meeting to convene in the tenth month next; but a considerable ~~nu~~ number of Friends dissenting from those measures and desirous of continuing the Quarterly Meeting in its connexion with the Yearly Meeting, remained together after the Seceders had withdrawn, and appointed John W. Balderston Clerk.

The following ~~named~~ Friends were named to assist the Clerk in preparing a minute more fully explanatory of the circumstances which have led to the present affecting state of things among us; viz, Isaac Chapman and Aaron Eastburn and report to an adjourned sitting of this Meeting to-morrow morning.

Then adjourned to ten o'clock to-morrow morning.

1827 – 8th mo. 31st About the time adjourned to, the Meeting again assembled.

The Friends appointed to prepare an explanatory minute produced the following; viz,

With feelings of deep concern and regret, we have observed a disposition manifesting itself in our Quarterly Meeting to depart from the salutary order of our Discipline and the requisite subordination to the Yearly Meeting, which for more than one hundred years has happily preserved us in unity among ourselves and in harmonious connexion with that Meeting: Of latter time this disposition has been painfully obvious in acts repugnant to the order of Society, and altogether subversive of the subordination necessary for the due support and preservation of all well regulated Communities: Contrary to former custom a large number of those appoint-

ed

(2)

1827. ed Representatives to our last Yearly Meeting, reported
8mo. in writing to our Quarter in the fifth month last, wherein they
arraign the Yearly Meeting, exhibiting several charges of misconduct without as we apprehend any just foundation, and
concluding by stating it as their judgment that it would
be unsafe to receive a Committee which had been appointed by that Meeting to visit the Quarterly and Monthly
Meetings; or to read the extracts from the minutes of said
Meeting; or in any other manner to acknowledge its authority:
This report was recorded on the minutes and a copy sent to
the respective Monthly Meetings; and in conformity with its
recommendation, the Committee of the Yearly Meeting who
were attending with a minute, were rejected, and the minute of their appointment, as also the extracts, refused to be
read. And in the Meeting held yesterday, to the pain
and grief of well concerned minds, much disorderly conduct
was manifested, and the same disposition evinced to
disregard the order of the Discipline: One of the Monthly Meetings belonging to a neighbouring Quarterly Meeting
without its consent, and whilst under its care for infractions of the Discipline, and without consulting said Quarter, was received and acknowledged as a component part
of that Meeting: A printed Address was read from a
number of members of Society convened in the City of Philadelphia proposing to establish a Meeting to be held in the
tenth month next in that place under the name of a
Yearly Meeting; this proposition was adopted and Representatives appointed to attend the same. Thus completely dissolving as far as these measures can dissolve the
connexion with and subordination to our Yearly Meeting, which
has so long, so beneficially and so harmoniously existed.
These measures were remonstrated against by a considerable number of Friends; but it was apparent that there was
a fixed determination on the part of others to carry their precon-
certed plans into execution. In which unpleasant situation
no alternative presented to the Friends of good order and sound
principles, than to remain together after the Separatists had
withdrawn

(3)

1827. withdrawn, and continue Bucks Quarterly Meeting on its origi=
8 mo. nal foundation, as a component part of, and in subordination to
our Yearly Meeting as heretofore held in Philadelphia."

Which was read, considered and united with.

The following copy of a minute of our last Yearly Mee=
ting was received and read; viz,

"At a Yearly Meeting held in Philadelphia by ad=
journments from the sixteenth of the fourth month to the
twenty first of the same inclusive 1827.

An exercise spreading and prevailing on account of the
present state of our Religious Society, and this Meeting be=
ing informed that our Women's Meeting have concluded to
appoint a Committee to visit the Quarterly and Monthly
Meetings as way may open, to unite with them therein for
the strength and assistance of those Meetings in the due support
of our salutary order and Discipline; the following Friends
are named, and the respective Meetings are desired to accommodate the Committee by making such adjournments as may
be needful to facilitate the performance of the service; viz,
Hinchman Haines, Abraham Pennell, Jonathan Evans,
Thomas Wistar, Samuel Bettle, Joseph Whitall, Thomas
Stewardson, Benjamin Cooper, Christopher Healy, William
Jackson, William Newbold, Edward Temple, Charles Shoemaker
and John Comfort (of Solebury).

Extracted from the minutes,

Samuel Bettle Clerk."

Most of whom were present, with whose company and
labours among us, a cordial sense of unity and acceptance was
expressed and felt.

Our Friend, Stephen Grellet, being on a religious visit
within the limits of those Quarterly Meetings west of the
Delaware that belong to our Yearly Meeting, very acceptably attended this Meeting, and produced a minute from Burlington
Monthly Meeting where he belongs, expressive of their full con=
currence with him therein.

Women Friends informed this Meeting, that a concern
had spread over their Meeting, to appoint a Committee to visit
(advise

314 1827

Epistle from the Yearly Meeting in the 10th Mo.

One hundred printed copies of an Epistle from our Yearly Meeting held in Philadelphia in the 10 month were received for distribution at our last Monthly Meeting, & a copy thereof was then read, which claiming the attention of this meeting, the Clerk is directed to record it with the minutes thereof.

An
Epistle
from the
Yearly Meeting of Friends
Held in Philadelphia
by adjournments from the 15th of the 10th Mo. to the 19th of the same, inclusive, 1827, to the Quarterly, Monthly, & Particular meetings of Friends within the compass of the said Yearly Meeting

Dear Friends

Having convened in this Yearly Meeting, under very peculiar and trying circumstances, in order to transact the business of the Church, our minds have been comforted & strengthened, in the evidence afforded that we are still mercifully regarded by our Holy Head, whose heavenly wing has graciously overshadowed this meeting to the humbling of our spirits, & tender sympathy has flowed towards our absent brethren & sisters, whom we affectionately salute in the love of the everlasting Gospel.

We fervently desire that all may be

12 Mo. 1827 " increasingly concerned to retire from the noises, the contentions, and
" the confusions that are in the world — that we may individually
" submit to the government of the Prince of Peace, who gathered our
" forefathers to be a people and committed to them important
" testimonies.
" These testimonies have been felt to be near & dear to us
" & a living travail has been known that our Zion may arise
" & shine in her ancient brightness, as in the morning of the
" day, when her sons & her daughters were despised & persecuted
" yet inherited the blessing pronounced by our Divine
" Master: "Blessed are ye when men shall revile you, and
" persecute you, and shall say all manner of evil against you,
" falsely, for my sake".
" Beloved friends, we feel the awful responsi-
" bility of our present standing, and the necessity of abiding,
" individually, in the meekness and simplicity of the Truth
" as it is in Jesus.. avoiding all doubtful disputations which
" engender strife, and earnestly endeavouring to show forth by
" a Godly life & conversation, that we are his humble followers,
" who, "when he was reviled, reviled not again", and whose
" religion enjoins that we resist not evil but overcome evil
" with good.
" We believe there never was a period in our
" Society, when it was more important for those who feel
" bound to the law and the testimony, to stand faithful at
" their posts; having on "the whole armour of God", which
" only can protect from the dangers that surround us. But
" if we keep a single eye to the Captain of our salvation,
" humbly waiting for him to put forth and go before us,
" we have nothing to fear — hard things will be made easy, and
" bitter things sweet; for "greater is he that is in you, than he that is
" in the world".

12 Mo. 1827

316.

In the present agitated state of society its living members must be led into exercise & suffering; and we earnestly desire that all may be preserved in the spirit of patience, gentleness, and forbearance under every provocation & trial. And, in the exercise of the salutary Discipline of the Church, Oh! that we may seek for a right qualification to treat with offenders in the spirit of restoring love, — most carefully guarding against the influence of party feeling, which may, almost imperceptibly, entwine itself into movements professedly designed to support the Discipline of Society. Let us remember that its original and primary object is, to seek & to save- not to destroy. If we in a spirit of violence seize the Discipline as a sword, to be wielded in the will & wisdom of man, we thereby depart from our ancient & Christian Principal, and wound the cause of truth & righteousness.

Our profession is high & holy; and let us be increasingly concerned to walk consistently therewith. The patient sufferings of our faithful predecessors finally established for them, an excellent name, even amongst their persecutors. They held up with practical clearness a peaceable testimony against "wars & fightings," and by scrupulous adherence to the principles of justice, became proverbial for their integrity.

In the present afflicting state of things, we feel deeply concerned that their example in these respects may be kept steadily in view — that our religious testimony may never be wounded by contending for property and asserting our rights; — that no course be pursued

12mo 1827

"although sanctioned by the laws of the excellent civil Government under which we live, that may be at variance with the Spirit of that holy Lawgiver, who taught his disciples, "If any man sue thee at the law and take away thy coat, let him have thy cloak also;" and who set forth his own situation as it related to this world when he said, "The foxes have holes, and the birds of the air have nests, but the son of man hath not where to lay his head."

And we tenderly exhort that in all places where our members constitute the larger part of any meeting, their conduct may be regulated by the rule laid down by our blessed Lord: "Whatsoever ye would that men should do to you do ye even so to them."

The Discipline under which we act, positively discourages members of our Society from suing each other at law. To violate this Discipline in a meeting capacity is not only a departure from our established order, but is calculated to injure us in the eyes of sober enquirers after truth, and to disturb the peace of our own minds.

Dearly beloved young friends! how shall we address you in language sufficiently impressive of the tender solicitude which we feel for your welfare! We are fully aware that many of you have witnessed scenes of contention, painfully affecting to the inexperienced mind, & calculated to produce the enquiry, "Who shall show us any good"? But remember, dear children, that truth is truth though all men forsake it. "The foundation of God standeth sure, having this seal, the Lord knoweth them that are his." although there may have been seasons when, as amidst the raging of the billows, you have been ready to cry out, Lord save us or we perish,

12 Mo 1827
318

" Yet you may remember that the Almighty Power which
" rebuked the winds and the waves, is the same that
" ever it was, and is still graciously disposed to say to
" to the humble tossed mind, "Peace, be still".
" Retire then, we entreat you, from all airy
" speculations on religious subjects—from all light &
" chaffy conversation. Enter into your closets—shut the
" door—commune with your own hearts and be still.
" Thus you will learn in the school of Christ. Your
" religious experience will be gradually enlarged, and
" as you continue humble & obedient you will be raised
" up a righteous generation, and will stand as faithful
" advocates for the law and the testimony of our God.
" There will arise from amongst you judges as at the
" first, and counsellors as at the beginning: insted
" of the fathers there will be the sons, and instead of
" the mothers there will be the daughters.
" The language of the Meeting for sufferings, in
" the introduction to the Book of Advices published
" under the direction of our Yearly Meeting in 1808,
" appears peculiarly adapted to our present situation
" and is as follows:
" "The following extracts have been compiled
" for the benefit of the members of our Yearly Meeting,
" that observing the travail of the Church under
" various concerns, which in divine wisdom have
" been communicated for its weighty attention, they
" may be drawn to the principle of Life & Light manifes
" ted in the mind, which points out the path of duty
" and can alone preserve therein.
" Our ancient Friends & their faithful

12 Mo. 1827 319

"successors to the present day have earnestly laboured to
"turn the attention of all to this pure spirit; knowing from
"experience, that it is the means appointed by God for
"effecting our salvation, and the only foundation of all
"true religion & worship. As by this we have been led
"into divers testimonies which have distinguished us
"from most other professors of the Christian name, we
"fervently desire that all our members may walk by
"the same rule & mind the same thing; thus every one
"filling his place in the body, we shall grow up into
"Him in all things, who is the Head, even Christ."

We recommend these advices to the weighty attention of all our members.

Finally, beloved friends, may we all remember that the Gospel of Christ stands not in speculative opinions, nor in the will and wisdom of man, but in the power of the one true & living God. Our blessed Lord gave ample proof of its simplicity, in electing illiterate fishermen to be amongst its promulgators. And as we are engaged humbly to abide in this power no divination nor enchantment can prevail against us. — "Now unto him that is able to keep you from falling, & to present you faultless before the presence of his glory with exceeding joy, to the only wise God our Saviour, be glory & majesty, dominion & power, both now and ever. Amen."

Signed by direction & on behalf of the meeting,
by Benjamin Ferris, Clerk of the men's meeting
Rebecca B Comly Clerk of the women's meeting

For the information of Friends, the Clerk was directed to add that the Yearly Meeting adjourned to meet again, in the city of

The Philadelphia Yearly Meeting Epistle of October 1827 (Hicksite)

Members of Plumpstead Preparative Meeting at time of Separation

Name	Friends	Hicksites	Neutrals	Fr. Ch.	Hs. do.	N. do.
A. Lydia Anderson		1				
3 B. William Bradshaw		1				
Susanna Bradshaw		1				
~~[illegible]~~						
Sarah Bradshaw		1			5	
Moses Bradshaw		1				
Eleanor Bradshaw		1			5	
John Brock		1				
Massy Brock		1				
Elizabeth Brock		1				
Mary Brock		1				
Samuel Brown		1				
Mary Brown		1			5	
Thomas Brown		1				
Sarah Brown		1			1	
Deborah Brown		1				
Joseph Burges		1				
Rachel Burges		1				
John Burges		1				
Elizabeth Burges			1			1
Hiram Burges		1				
Catharine Burges		1			1	
Aaron Burges		1				
Esther Burges		1			2	
Rachel Burges Widow		1				
~~Rebecca Burges~~						
~~Wife of Jn. Burges jr~~						
3						
Mellicent Carr		1				
C. Daniel Carlile	1					
Elizabeth Carlile	1					
Benjamin Carlile		1			3	
Elisha Carlile		1				
Jonathan Carr		1			7	
Miriam Carr Widow		1				
Eli Cadwallader		1				
Rachel Cadwallader		1			4	
Peter Cadwallader		1				
David Cadwallader		1				
Cyrus Cadwallader		1				
Rebecca Cadwallader	1					1

Name	Friends	Hicksites	Neutrals	Fr. Ch.	Hs. do.	N. do.
C. Elias Carey			1			
Hannah Carey			1			
Jonathan Child	1					
Deborah Child	1			1		
Isaac Child	1					
Rachel Child		1				
Israel Child	1					
D. Joseph Duer		1				
Sarah Duer	1					4
Ann Duer		1				
Mary Dyer	1					
Sarah Dyer	1					
Jemima Dyer	1					
Rachel Dyer	1					
Elizabeth B. Dyer	1					
Mary Doan Widow		1				
F. John Fell	1					
Edith Fell	1					
Samuel Fell						
Hannah Fell	1					
Martha Fell	1					
Jane S. Fell	1					
Martha Fell			1			4
Mary Fell			1			
Elizabeth Fell			1			
Eli Fell		1				
Rachel Fell		1			7	
Sarah Fell	1					
Mary Fenton		1				
G. John Good		1			5	
Nathan Good		1				
Eleanor Good		1				
Jane Good		1				
H. Jacob Hutchins			1			
Isaac Hutchins			1			

Members of Plumpstead Preparative Meeting Continued

Friends | Hicksites | Neutrals | Sr. Ch. | Jr. Ch. | N. ?

J. Jesse Jones
Sarah Jones
Hiram Jones
Amos Jones

K. Mary Kirkbride Widow
Sarah Kirkbride
Grace Mitchener
~~Mary Mitchener~~
Ruth Meredith
M. Mary Mitchener Widow
Isaiah Mitchener
Margaret Mitchener
Hannah Mitchener
George Mitchener
Hannah Mitchener
Hannah Mitchener Jun.
Joshua Mitchener
Elizabeth Mitchener
John Mitchener
Esther Mitchener
John S. Mitchener
Harriet B. Mitchener
Josiah Mitchener
Abraham Mitchener
Jane Mitchener
Marmaduke Mitchener
Hannah Mitchener
Samuel Mitchener
John Mitchener Tanner
Rebecca Mitchener
Jemima Mitchener
Martha Mitchener
Elliott Mitchener
Joseph Moore
Jane Moore
Ann Moore
James Moore
Elizabeth Meredith

P. John Poulton
Mary Poulton
Leah Painter
Ann Preston
Deborah Preston
Euphemia Preston

P. Silas Preston
Margaret Preston
Martha Preston
Elizabeth Price

R. Alexander Rich
Mary Rich
John Rich
Rachel Rich
Joseph Rich
Deborah Robinson
Elizabeth Robinson
Cephas Ross
Mary Ross
S. Jonathan Shaw
James Shaw
Hannah Shaw
Joseph Shaw
Alexander Shaw
Martha Shaw
Sarah Shaw
Hannah Shaw
John Shaw
Martha Shaw
Rachel Shaw
Sarah Shaw
~~Robert Shaw~~
John Shaw
Grace Shaw
Hannah Shaw Wife of Jas.
Ann Shaw
Susanna Shaw Wife of Aaron
Sarah Strawn Widow
Sarah Shepherd Widow
Timothy Smith
Rachel Smith
Jervis Smith
Mahlon Smith
Deborah Smith
Daniel Smith
Hannah Smith
Albert Smith
Elizabeth Smith
George Smith
Mary Smith
Rachel Smith Wife of Wm.

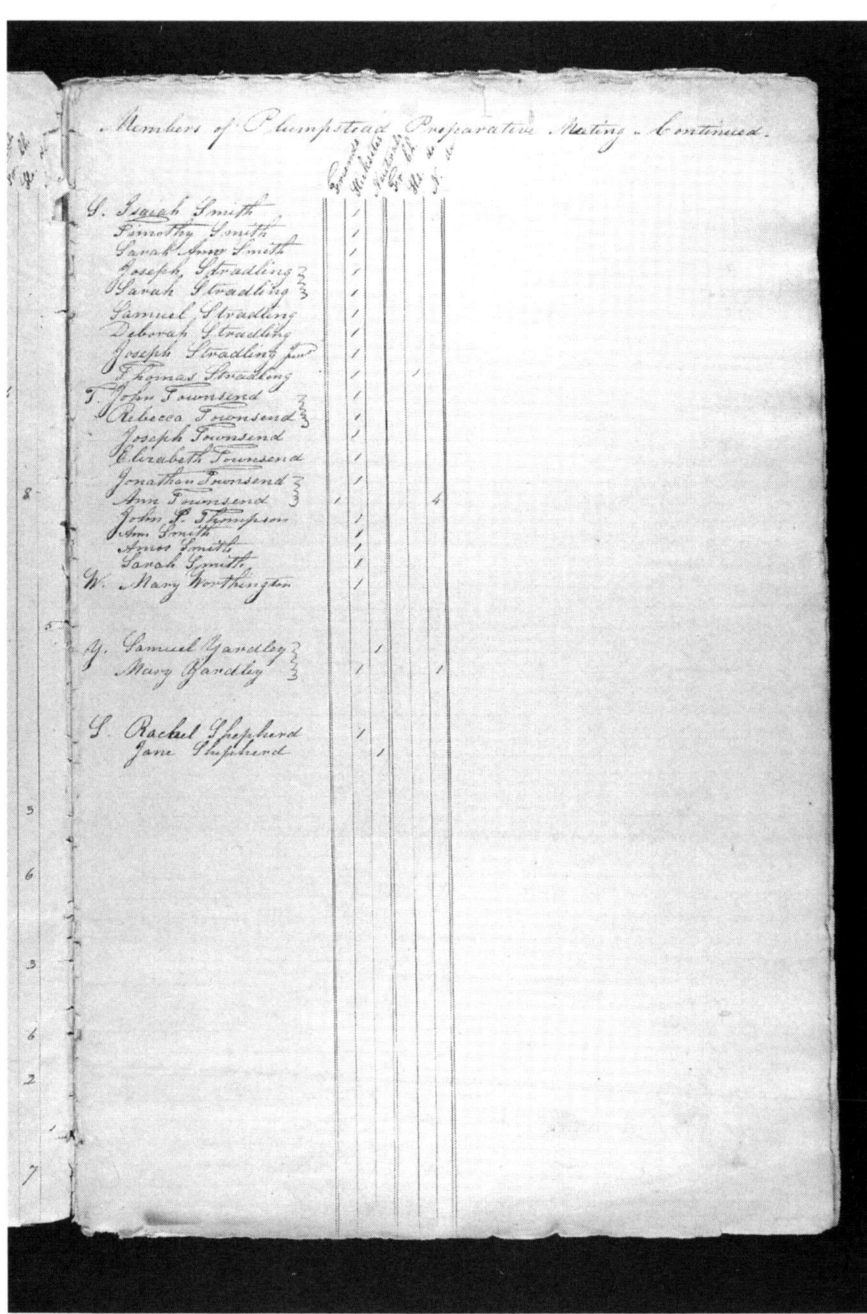

Members of Plumpstead Preparative Meeting – Continued.

	Name	Friends	Hicksites	Neutrals	Fr. Ch.	Hs. do	N. do
S.	Isaiah Smith		1				
	Timothy Smith		1				
	Sarah Ann Smith		1				
	Joseph Stradling		1				
	Sarah Stradling		1				
	Samuel Stradling		1				
	Deborah Stradling		1				
	Joseph Stradling Junr		1				
	Thomas Stradling		1			1	
T.	John Townsend		1				
	Rebecca Townsend		1				
	Joseph Townsend		1				
	Elizabeth Townsend		1				
	Jonathan Townsend		1				
	Ann Townsend	1					4
	John S. Thompson		1				
	Ann Smith		1				
	Amos Smith		1				
	Sarah Smith		1				
W.	Mary Worthington		1				
Y.	Samuel Yardley			1			
	Mary Yardley		1				1
S.	Rachel Shepherd		1				
	Jane Shepherd			1			

A complete list of Plumstead Meeting members in 1827 and their affiliations

[No. 1.] ENUMERATION an

Names of Owners of Real Property.	By whom Occupied.	Seated Lands. Number of Acres.	Seated Lands. Value per Acre. Dols.	Seated Lands. Gross actual Value, including improvements, such as Houses, Barns, Furnaces, Forges, Foundries, Bloomeries, Distilleries, Breweries, Tan Yards, Mills, and Manufactories of all descriptions. Dols.	Unseated Lands. Number of Acres.	Unseated Lands. Gross actual Value. Dols.
William S. Michener		71	25	1725		
Elias Maslin		5		200		
Edward & Sarah Michener		75	30	2250		
John Mast		47	18	846		
David G. Moyers		11½	60	690		
Nathan L. Malsbury		11½	60	690		
John F. & Reuben M. Moyers		84	28	2352		
Reuben F. Moyers		88	24	2112		
John Maslin		5	60	300		
John Moyers ma.		102	22	2244		
George F. Michener		22	50	1100		
Christn & Jacob Moyers		113 6 10 4 13	40 30 20 16 8	4520 180 200 64 108		
Society of Friends of Plumstead Meeting		10	40	400		

The 1859 Bucks County tax record showing Plumstead Meeting paying taxes on 10 acres out of the 15 acre property. Construction of the tenant house in 1855 converted the land to a "seated" category and a higher tax rate.

124. | 125.

What is the No. of the following descriptions belonging to Buckingham Monthly Meeting

Families	Heads of families	Male adults	Female adults	male minors aged 15 years & upwards	female minors aged 15 years & upwards	male minors aged between 5 & 15 yrs	female minors aged between 5 & 15 yrs	male minors aged 5 yrs & under	female minors aged 5 yrs & under	Total
Buckingham Preparative Meeting is composed of										
60	61	90	115	10	15	13	16	11	7	278
Plumstead Preparative Meeting is composed of										
38	14	34	40	4	2	4	5	2	2	93
Buckingham Monthly Meeting is composed of										
118	75	124	155	14	17	17	21	13	9	371

What is the No. of minors amongst Friends within the limits of the same monthly meeting where one parent is a member and the said minors are not members.

Buckingham Preparative Meeting	17	10	28	23	14	18	110
Plumstead Preparative meeting	2	6	6	7	4	3	28
Buckingham Monthly Meeting	19	16	34	30	18	21	138

The committee to visit Mary B. Michener and Mary B. Michener two minor children report they have attended [illegible]

assistance of a Presbyterian Minister, with a man in membership with another religious denomination [illegible]

205.

The friends appointed to prepare a list of the members formerly belonging to Plumstead Preparative Meeting produced the following

"Sixth Mo. 7th 1867

List of Members belonging to Plumstead Meeting

Aaron Burgess
John D Burgess
Joseph Burgess
Geo. Childs
James Cadwallader
Eli Cadwallader
Charles Cadwallader
David Carr
Eli Fell
Geo. B. Fell
William Heacock
Samuel Hart
Isaiah Michener
Ezra Michener
Curtis Michener
Horace Michener
Elliot Michener
Cornly Michener
Burroughs Michener
Thomas Stradling
Joseph Stradling
Mahlon Smith
Jonas Smith
Alexander Shaw
John S Thompson
Charles Thompson
Lewis B Thompson
Esther Burgess
Ann D Burges
Mary T Burges
Martha Burges
Elizabeth Carlisle
Millicent Carr
Christiana Cadwallader

Elizabeth Carver
Mary Ann Doughty
Elizabeth Fell
Miriam Fell
Mary Ellen Fell
Ury B Gibson
Lavina Heacock
Evelina Heacock
Grace Haldeman
Elizabeth Hockman
Amanda Hinkle
Anna Hudnut
Sarah Hall
Hannah Michener
Esther Michener
Mary B Michener
Caroline C Michener
Jemima Michener
Martha Michener
Annie M Michener
Jane Moore
Eunice Poulton
Elizabeth Poulton
Martha Preston
Sallie Paxson
Mary W Phillips
Elizabeth Smith
Rebecca Smith
Gainor T Smith
Mary Stradling
Grace Shaw
Mary Ann Shaw
Hannah Shaw
Mary M Stradling

Mary Anna Stradling
Margaret Thompson
Caroline Elizabeth Watson
Margaret P Childs

Minors

Stacy Cadwallader
Howard Cadwallader
[illegible] Cadwallader
Charles Michener
Anson B Michener
Edmund C Michener

Rachel Ann Cadwallader
Clarissa J Michener
Henrietta Shaw "

In the year 1875 the second Meeting House was rebuilt. From the minutes of Buckingham Monthly Meeting of Friends, 4th Mo. 10th, 1875 there is a detailed statement of the cost of the rebuilding, which was $1308.13. A photostatic copy has been made of this statement and appears on another page of this booklet. It is interesting to note the names of the donors for this project, also the expenditures, and at the foot of the page we learn that most of the actual work was done by members of the Meeting without charge.

On 5th Mo. 3rd, 1875 the trustees of Plumstead Meeting were given permission to sell part of their land to raise money for the rebuilding of the second Meeting House. Two parcels were sold as follows:

4 acres 56 perches to John Shafer for $550.00
1 acre 100 perches to Isaac Myers for $220.00

From information obtained from the Plumstead Preparative minutes it was learned that members supported the education of their children by a General Subscription Fund for school purposes. In March, 1855 public schools were established and the subscription fund was then used to erect a small stone tenant house for the caretaker of the Meeting; the cost of which was given as $525.10, most of the work being done by members.

In reading through the Buckingham Monthly Meeting minutes from 1720, these facts were disclosed:

On 3rd Mo. 3rd, 1730 Plumstead Friends made a request to Buckingham Monthly Meeting of Friends as follows: "That they might make application to the Quarterly Meeting for a Meeting among themselves, with this Meeting (Buckingham) for a comfort, and the Meeting allows that they may make application to the Quarterly Meeting upon that account." This request was approved.

On 4th Mo. 5th, 1824 Plumstead Preparative Meeting requested "Buckingham Meeting to take into consideration the expediency of setting up a Monthly Meeting at Plumstead, to be composed of part of Buckingham Monthly Meeting." Buckingham Meeting was

We, the Committee appointed by Buckingham Monthly meeting of Friends to superintend the re-erection of Plumstead Friends meeting house, make the following report

Dr. report of Comly Michener Treasurer of Building Committee –

Received of John Shaffer for four acres and 456 perches of woodland belonging to said meeting	550	00
Rec'd of Isaac Meyers for one (1) acre and one hundred (100) perches of woodland belonging to the aforsaid –	200	00
Donation from Henry P. Darlington	10	00
" " Margaret Ball of [illegible]	10	00
Old lumber, Stone &c, Sold	79	32
Frank Preston for window lights &c	13	92
Received of Abner Walton from Buckingham Monthly meeting –	400	00
Donation from Thomas Stradling	10	00
Donation from Martha Ann Michener	5	00
1882 9th mo 1st Received $29.89 rent of tenant house on meeting grounds	29	89
	$1308	13

Building Committee { Comly Michener, Abner Walton, Ezra Michener

4th Mo. 10th 1875.

Cr. report of Comly Michener, Treasurer of Building Committee.

Paid J. Watson Case for surveying as per receipt		3	00
Paid Harper Hellerman as per. contract		[illegible]	00
" " " for Extra work		7[illegible]	56
Paid Jacob R. Lear, as per. contract		290	00
" " " for extra work		35	75
Paid G. & H. Lear,			
for Professional services,	15.00		
Auditors Fees &c	14.95		
Prothonatary's Fees	4.50		
		34	45
Paid H. T. Darlington, for advertising		9	10
" W. W. H. Davis, " "		4	[illegible]
" Lewis Hofford, date stone		7	[illegible]
" Elias Benner, sill stone,		2	38
" William Tinsman for lumber &c		6	22
" Robt. McCroasdale & Son, for painting		62	[illegible]
" Jacob Constantine, for labor,		2	16
" D. Gotwals & Sons, Store bill		33	32
" Trumbower & Murfit, lumber.		101	82
" John Edwards, for labor –		3	69
" Frank Preston, spouting &c		11	67
		$1318	19

The hauling of sand, lime and lumber, casting stone, grading &c was done by the members and friends of the meeting and time spent by the committee all without charge.

in favor of this request and referred the matter to the Quarterly Meeting.

The report from Quarterly Meeting on 9th Mo. 6th, 1824 was as follows: "We of the committee appointed to take into consideration the propriety of establishing a Monthly Meeting at Plumstead, having several times met and deliberated thereon, agree to report that way does not open with sufficient clearness to us to recommend the establishment of a Monthly Meeting at that place at the present time."

Plumstead Meeting never became a Monthly Meeting.

On 4th Mo. 4th, 1864 the Plumstead Friends reported that their mid-week and Preparative Meetings were so small, they believed the time had come to discontinue them. This matter was referred to Quarterly Meeting for its consideration. Late in 1864 Quarterly Meeting, after careful consideration of the subject, deemed it wise to discontinue further Plumstead Meetings. However, Meetings were continued off and on until 1869 and the following is a quotation from Buckingham minutes of 4th Mo. 5th, 1869: "The following is a copy of a minute in relation to Plumstead Meeting received from our Quarterly Meeting. Wrightstown 2 Mo. 25th, 1869 — the matter as contained in the report from Buckingham Monthly Meeting was, after deliberate consideration united with by the Meeting, Women's Meeting also uniting herein, the said Meeting (Plumstead) is therefore discontinued and the members attached to Buckingham Preparative Meeting. The clerks are directed to forward information thereof to Buckingham Monthly Meeting."

Signed: Barclay Knight
Rachel Palmer, Clerks.

Aaron Burgess and Comly Michener were appointed to furnish Buckingham Monthly Meeting with a list of the names of all who were members of Plumstead Preparative Meeting.

* * * * *

The following is a list of Plumstead members transferred to Buckingham Monthly Meeting, dated 6 Mo. 7th, 1869:

294.

Representatives — To attend the ensuing Quarterly Meeting as our Representatives [illegible] K Scarborough Comly Michener and Benj W Smith were appointed.

The friends to audit the accounts of the Plumstead Building Committee Reported in writing as follows;

Audit Building Com. Plumstead Meeting house — "The friends appointed to audit the accounts of the Building Committee for Plumstead "Meeting house have attended to the duties "assigned them, having examined their "vouchers and found them correct,

"The whole cost of rebuilding being One thousand "three hundred & Eight Dolls and thirteen cents " $1308.13

"The Building Committee have collected from
"Real Estate sold Seven hundred & fifty Dolls (750.00)
"Old Lumber and Stone sold Ninety three 24/100 Dols (93.24)
" Donations Seventeen (17.00)
"Making Eight hundred & Sixty four 24/100 Dolls 860.24

" This amount has been paid over for materials "found and to the contractors, leaving a "balance yet unpaid of Four hundred & "Forty Seven 89/100 Dolls (447.89)

The meeting accepted this report and directs that the fund arising from the sale of wood from the premises of Buckingham Meeting be appropriated to the liquidation of the Balance yet due

M. S. Fell Certificate — A Certificate recommending Martha S Fell to the Phila Monthly Meeting of Friends on Green Street, was read, approved and directed to be signed and returned to Women Friends for further care

Treasurers account — To settle the treasurers account, ascertain what money will be required the ensuing year, and if any to assess and collect it Abner Walton Samuel K Rice, Benj W Smith & Comly Michener were appointed.

Buckingham Preparative Meeting minutes detailing the account sheet for the 1875 rebuilding of the Plumstead meetinghouse.

BIBLIOGRAPHY

Barbour, Hugh. 1995. "Rationalists, Quietists and Universalists." In *Quaker Crosscurrents*, by Hugh Barbour, 100–106. Syracuse: Syracuse University Press.

Blanco, Richard L. 1981. "American Army Hospitals in Pennsylvania during the Revolutionary War." *Pennsylvania History*, October 1: 347–368.

Bradley, A. D. 1987. "The Journal of John Churchman: A Wartime Publication." *Quaker History*, Spring: 62–65.

Brinton, Howard H. 1988. *Friends for 300 Years.* Wallingford: Pendle Hill Publications.

Bronner, Edwin B. 1981. "A Time of Change." In *Friends in the Delaware Valley*, by John M. Moore, 103-137. Haverford: Friends Historical Association.

Cadbury, Henry J. 1938. "Quaker Relief During the Siege of Boston." *Transactions of the Colonial Society of Massachusetts 1937-1942*, April.

Caton, Anne Marie. 2003. "The Aesthetics of Absence: Quaker Women's Plain Dress in the Delaware Valley 1790-1900." In *Quaker Aesthetics*, by Emma Lapsansky and Anne Verplanck, 246-271. Philadelphia: University of Pennsylvania.

Common Schools of Pennsylvania. 1878. *Report of the Superintendent of Public Instruction of the Commonwealth of Pennsylvania.* Harrisburg: Lane S. Hart.

Commonwealth of Pennsylvania. n.d. *Crossing the Alleghenies. Chapter One: Early Turnpikes and the Old State Road.* explorepahistory.com/story.php?storyId=1-9-A&chapter=1.

Crooks, Jesse. n.d. *The Testimony of Simplicity and Quaker Practices.* essay, unpublished.

Crothers, A. Glenn. 2018. "Review: Abraham Lincoln, the Quakers, and the Civil War by William C. Kashatus." *Journal of the Abraham Lincoln Association.* Summer. Accessed November 2, 2021. quod.lib.umich.edu/j/jala/2629860.0039.207/--abraham-lincoln-the-quakers-and-the-civil-war-a-trial?rgn=main;view=fulltext.

Davis, W.W.H. 1876. "Chapter XXIV: Plumstead Township." In *The History of Bucks County, Pennsylvania*, by W.W.H. Davis, 398-414. Doylestown: Democrat Book and Job Office Print.

Davis, W.W.H. 1905 (1975 reprint). "Chapter XXIV:Plumstead Township." In *The History of Bucks County Pennsylvania*, by W.W.H. Davis, 379-395. New York: The Lewis Publishing Company.

Davis, W.W.H. 1885. "Plumstead Township." In *Bucks County Historical Society Lectures, vol. 1*, 305-313. Doylestown: Bucks County Historical Society.

Day, Sherman. 1843 . *Excerpts from Historical Collections of the State of Pennsylvania.* reprinted by Doug Rebok.

Doylestown Intelligencer. 1854. "Improvement." October 31.

Doylestown Intelligencer. 1899. "Philanthropic Committee." September 21.

Doylestown Intelligencer. 1874. "Repairs Proposed." December 15.

Dyer, John. 1906. *Memoranda from the Journal of John Dyer.* Philadelphia: Genealogical Society of Pennsylvania.

Fell, Laura D. 1953. "Plumstead Friends Meetinghouse 225th Anniversary." booklet.

Friends Historical Library. n.d. *Quaker Burial Grounds in Philadelphia.* Accessed October 31, 2021. www.swarthmore.edu/library/friends/philaburials3.htm.

Frost, J. William. 2003. "From Plainness to Simplicity: Changing Quaker Ideals for Material Culture." In *Quaker Aesthetics*, by Emma Lapsansky and Anne Verplanck, 16-40. Philadelphia: University of Pennsylvania Press.

—. 2012. "Quaker Antislavery: From Dissidence to Sense of the Meeting." *Quaker History*, Spring: 12-23.

Frost, J. William. 1981. "Years of Crisis and Separation: Philadelphia Yearly Meeting 1790-1850." In *Friends in the Delaware Valley*, by John M. Moore, 57-102. Haverford: Friends Historical Association.

Haviland, R.S. 1891. "Visits and Meetings in Bucks County." *Friends Intelligencer and Journal*, March 21: 186-187.

Hicksite Friends. 1828. "Misstatements Corrected." *The Friend, or Advocate of Truth*, February: 47-56.

Hinshaw, Seth B. 2001. *The Evolution of Quaker Meetinghouses in North America 1670-2000.* thesis, Philadelphia: University of Pennsylvania.

Historic American Buildings Survey. 2002. *Silent Witness: Quaker Meetinghouses in the Delaware Valley, 1695 to the Present.* Philadelphia: Philadelphia Yearly Meeting.

Jones, Rufus. n.d. *The Faith and Practice of the Quakers.* Richmond: Friends United Press.

Jordan, John W. 1911. *Colonial and Revolutionary Families of Pennsylvania: Genealogical and Personal Memoirs.* New York: Lewis Publishing Company.

Kenderdine, Thaddeus. 1902. "Plumstead Meeting." *Friends Intelligencer*, November 29: 761-763.

Kirson, Alice Atkinson. 1923. *Buckingham Monthly Meeting.* Buckingham, PA: Buckingham Friends Meeting.

LaVO, Carl. 2020. "Carl LaVO: Forgotten Native American Towns of Bucks County." *Bucks County Courier Times.* November 23. Accessed October 27, 2021. www.buckscountycouriertimes.com/story/lifestyle/2020.

—. 2018. "Reconsidering the Outlaw Doan Gang." *The Doylestown Intelligencer*, July 30.

Levy, Barry. 1988. *Quakers and the American Family.* New York: Oxford University Press.

Long Island Community Foundation. 2003. *Elias Hicks, Quaker Preacher.* Accessed October 31, 2021. www.westburyquakers.org/qt/archive/files/EliasHicks.htm.

MacReynolds, George. 1976. *Place Names in Bucks County.* Doylestown: Bucks County Historical Society.

Mann, Charles C. 2011. *1491.* New York: Vintage Books.

Marietta, Jack D. 1984. *The Reformation of American Quakerism 1748-1783.* Philadelphia: University of Pennsylvania Press.

Matlack, T. Chalkley. 1938. *Brief Historical Sketches Concerning Friends Meetings of the Past and Present.* manuscript, unpublished.

Matlack, T. Chalkley. 1938. *Friends Meetinghouses in Pennsylvania.* notebook, unpublished.

McNealy, Terry. 2002. *Bucks County, An Illustrated History.* Doylestown: Bucks Cunty Historical Society.

Mekeel, Arthur J. 1981. "The Founding Years." In *Friends in the Delaware Valley*, by John M. Moore, 13-56. Haverford: Friends Historical Association.

—. 1976. "Quaker History." *The Relation of Quakers to the American Revolution*, Spring: 3-18.

Michener, Comly. 1965. *Plumstead Friends Meeting Burial Grounds: A Brief History and Index of Graves.* booklet, unpublished.

National Park Service. 1997. "Meetinghouse." *Buckingham Friends Meeting.* Accessed October 28, 2021. www.buckinghamfriendsmeeting.org/Home/meetinghouse.

National Register of Historic Places. 1991. "Gardenville Rural Historical District." *Wikipedia: Gardenville North Branch Rural Historic District.* January. Accessed November 1, 2021. www.gis.penndot.gov/CRGISAttachments/SiteResource/H096572_01H.pdf.

Orthodox Friends. 1827. "Commentary." *The Friend*, December: 61-62.

Pearsy, Mark. 2018. "We Are Your Real Friends: The Exile of Quakers During the American Revolution and Teaching Contenious Issues." *Ohio Social Studies Review*, September 23: 36-46.

Pennsylvania Historical Survey. 1941. *Inventory of Church Archives: Society of Friends in Pennsylvania.* Philadelphia: Friends Historical Association.

Pennsylvania, Common Schools of. 1878. *Report of the Superintendent of Public Instruction of the Commonwealth of Pennsylvania* . Harrisburg: Lane S. Hart.

Philadelphia Yearly Meeting. 1824. *The Cabinet, or Works of Darkness Brought to Light.* Philadelphia: available through Quaker Heritage Press and online at www.qhpress.org/texts/h-p/cabinet.html.

Poole, Amy. 2010. "Spring Cleaning." *Early American LIfe* , April: 50-53.

Powers, John. 2006. *Growing Up Quaker in the Civil War.* thesis, Haverford: Haverford College.

Religious Society of Friends. 1998. *Faith and Practice- A Book of Christian Discipline.* Philadelphia: Philadelphia Yearly Meeting.

Religious Society of Friends. 2018. *Faith and Practice.* Philadelphia: Philadelphia Yearly Meeting.

Shaddinger, Anna E. 1958. *The Micheners in America.* Rutland: C.E. Tuttle Co. .

Soderlund, Jean R. 2015. *Lenape Country.* Philadelphia: University of Pennsylvania Press.

—. 1983. *William Penn and the Founding of Pennsylvania.* Philadelphia: University of Pennsylvania Press.

staff. 2016. "Milestones: Obituary of Maris Langford." *Friends Journal.* February 1. Accessed November 3, 2021. www.friendsjournal.org/milestones-february-2016/.

Verenna, Thomas. 2014. "Easton's Missing Dead." *Journal of the American Revolution*, August 12.

Whitman, Walt. 1888. "Anecdotes about Elias Hicks." *wikisource.* Accessed October 31, 2021. www.wikisource.org.

Wickersham, James P. 1886. *A History of Education in Pennsylvania.* Lancaster: Inquirer Publishing Company.

Wilbur, Henry W. 1910. *Life and Labors of Elias Hicks.* Philadelphia: Friends General Conference Advancement Committee.

ENDNOTES

Chapter One: Europeans Arrive in the Delaware Valley

i Soderlund, Lenape Country, p. 16

ii *Faith and Practice,* pp. 1–3

iii The letter appears in its entirety in Soderlund, *William Penn,* pp. 86–88

iv Soderlund, *William Penn*, p. 316

v Soderlund, *Lenape Country,* p. 197

vi Soderlund, *William Penn,* pp. 71-72

vii Soderlund, *Lenape,* p.172

viii Soderlund, *William Penn,* etc., p. 160. The Treaty appears in its entirety.

ix Levy, pp. 124,126

x Poole, p. 52

xi LaVO, "Forgotten Native American Towns"

xii Kirson, p. 2

xiii Davis, "Plumstead Township" in *Lectures,* p. 307

xiv Davis, *Lectures* pp. 305–306

xv Matthews, p. 312

xvi Davis, Lectures, p. 312

xvii Day, p. 156

xviii Wallace, p. 233

xix Commonwealth of Pennsylvania, "Early Turnpikes"

xx Matthews, p. 310

Vignette: Cephas Child

xxi Except where noted, this biography is based on Jordan, p. 1119

xxii Buckingham Monthly Meeting minutes 3rd d./5th mo./1756

Chapter Two: The Establishment of Plumstead Meeting

xxiii Levy, p. 237

xxiv Day, p. 157

xxv Davis, *History of Bucks County*, (1876) pp. 400–401

xxvi National Park Service, p. 14

xxvii Buckingham Monthly Meeting minutes, 7th d./7th mo./ 1727 (OS) & 3rd d./8th mo./ 1727 (OS)

xxviii Davis, *Lectures*, p. 310

xxix Buckingham Monthly Meeting minutes 7th d./2nd mo./1730 (OS)

xxx Buckingham Monthly Meeting minutes, 5th d./3rd mo./1730 (OS)

xxxi Buckingham Monthly Meeting minutes, 3rd d./9th mo./1730 (OS)

xxxii Buckingham Monthly Meeting minutes, 2nd d./12th mo./1730

xxxiii Davis, *Lectures*, p. 310

xxxiv Hinshaw, p. 30

xxxv Matthews, p. 71

xxxvi Buckingham Monthly Meeting minutes 7th d./1st mo./1754

xxxvii Kenderdine, p. 761

xxxviii Pennsylvania Historical Survey, p. 195

xxxix Hinshaw, p. 131. He also states that locating the facing benches other than on the north wall was all but unknown.

xl Buckingham Monthly Meeting minutes, 2nd d./3rd mo./1761

xli Brinton, p. 185

xlii Marietta, p. 156

xliii Philadelphia Yearly Meeting extracts as recorded in the Buckingham Monthly Meeting minutes 6th d./12th mo./1756

xliv Buckingham Monthly Meeting minutes 12th d./12th mo./1758

xlv Levy, p. 16

Chapter Three: Revolution

xlvi Dyer, journal entry for April 13, 1768

xlvii The Buckingham Monthly Meeting minutes for this period describe the meeting's location in the heading.

xlviii Buckingham Monthly Meeting minutes 6th d./1st mo./1772 xlix Cadbury, available online at www.colonialsociety.org/node/616#ah1002, no pages given.

l Buckingham Monthly Meeting minutes for 1st d./7th mo./1776

li Bucks Quarterly Meeting minutes and PYM epistle as recorded in the Buckingham Monthly Meeting minutes for 2nd d./12th mo./1776

lii Dyer, journal entry for August 11, 1777

liii Blanco, p. 359

liv Verenna, (available on line at www.allthingsliberty.com/2014/08/eastons-missing-dead/ pages not indicated)

lv Davis, W.W.H., in *History* (1905), p. 386

lvi Davis, W.W.H., "Plumstead Township" in *Lectures*, p. 310

lvii Marietta, p. 257

lviii Pearsy, p. 40

lix Bradley, p. 63

lx Buckingham Monthly Meeting minutes 1st d./2nd mo./1779

lxi Marietta, p. 252, 275

lxii Mekeel, "The Founding Years" in Moore, p. 53

lxiii LaVO, "Reconsidering the Outlaw Doan Gang"

lxiv McNealy, pp. 134, 135

Chapter Four: The State of the Church

lxv Brinton, p. 177

lxvi Hinshaw, p. 137

lxvii Jones, p. 62

lxviii Mekeel, "The Founding Years" in Moore, p. 38

lxix Marietta, p. 10

lxx Mekeel, "Founding" p. 38

lxxi Bucks Quarterly Meeting minutes 26th d./2nd mo./1756

lxxii Buckingham Monthly Meeting minutes 2nd d./2nd mo./1767. Bezenet's book had been published by Philadelphia Yearly Meeting.

lxxiii Buckingham Monthly Meeting minutes 1st d./1st mo./1768

lxxiv Moore, appendix prepared by Barbara I. Curtis, p. 261.

lxxv Buckingham Monthly Meeting minutes 3rd d./12th mo./1787

lxxvi Dyer, *Journal*, several entries in the month of October 1797

lxxvii Friends Historical Library, *Quaker Burial Grounds in Philadelphia*

lxxviii Barbour, p. 101

lxxix Frost, "Years" pp. 65–66
lxxx Frost, "From Plainness" p. 30
lxxxi Brinton, p. 97
lxxxii Frost, "Years" pp.71–72
lxxxiii Barbour, p. 106
lxxxiv Frost, "From Plainness" p. 30
lxxxv Long Island Community Foundation, "Elias Hicks, Quaker Preacher" website
lxxxvi Frost, "Years" p. 77
lxxxvii Barbour, pp. 121–123
lxxxviii Religious Society of Friends, *Faith and Practice* (2018), p. 87
lxxxix Frost, "Years," p. 74
xc Barbour, p. 125
xci Wilbur, p. 170
xcii Philadelphia Yearly Meeting, "The Cabinet" letter from ten Elders to Elias Hicks dated December 19, 1822.
xciii PYM, "Cabinet" letter from ten Elders to Elias Hicks dated January 4, 1823.
xciv Wilbur, pp. 139–151, describes these two years in more detail.
xcv Frost, "Years" p. 70
xcvi Philadelphia Yearly Meeting minutes April 17-21, 1826
xcvii Barbour, p. 125
xcviii Frost, "Years" p. 77
xcix Brinton, p. 97
c Whitman, online at wikisource.org

Vignette: Regarding Elias Hicks

ci Philadelphia Yearly Meeting, "The Cabinet" letter from Thomas Eddy to John Warder dated October 18, 1822

Chapter Five: Plumstead Divided

cii Buckingham Monthly Meeting minutes 3rd d./5th mo./1824
ciii Buckingham Monthly Meeting minutes 6th d./9th mo./1824
civ Buckingham Monthly Meeting minutes 1st d./4th mo./1799
cv Buckingham Monthly Meeting minutes 7th d./5th mo./1827 (contains the entire epistle)
cvi Buckingham Monthly Meeting minutes 4th d./6th mo./1827

cvii Buckingham Monthly Meeting minutes 2nd d./7th mo./1827
cviii Hicksite Friends, "Misstatements Corrected" p. 48
cix Hicksite Friends, "Misstatements Corrected" p. 48
cx Buckingham Monthly Meeting minutes 3rd d./9th mo./1827
cxi Hicksite Friends, "Misstatements" p. 48
cxii Hicksite Friends, "Misstatements" p. 51
cxiii Buckingham Monthly Meeting minutes 1st d./10th mo./1827
cxiv Hicksite Friends, "Misstatements" p. 51
cxv Hicksite Friends, "Misstatements" p. 53
cxvi Orthodox Friends, "Commentary" p. 62
cxvii Bucks Quarterly Meeting minutes 29th d./11th mo./1827
cxviii Bucks Quarterly Meeting enumeration book, pp. 21-23. See images in appendix.
cxix Buckingham Orthodox Monthly Meeting minutes 5th d./8th mo./1866, a report as to the status of things thirty-nine years earlier
cxx Buckingham Orthodox Monthly Meeting minutes 5th d./1st mo./1828
cxxi Buckingham Hicksite Monthly Meeting minutes 5th d./1st mo./1835
cxxii Buckingham Hicksite Monthly Meeting minutes 7th d./12th mo./1835
cxxiii National Register of Historic Places, "Gardenville" section 7, p. 2
cxxiv Matthews, p. 1
cxxv Buckingham Hicksite Monthly Meeting minutes 2nd d./11th mo./1835, and 8th d./11th mo./1838
cxxvi Buckingham Hicksite Monthly Meeting minutes 3rd d./5th mo./1852
cxxvii Buckingham Hicksite Monthly Meeting minutes 1st d./3rd mo./1852
cxxviii Hinshaw, p. 153
cxxix "Improvement" 1854
cxxx Buckingham Hicksite Monthly Meeting minutes 3rd d./11th mo./1862. See appendix
cxxxi Buckingham Hicksite Monthly Meeting minutes 4th mo./5th d./1869
cxxxii Fell, pp. 13–14

Vignette: Plumstead Orthodox Meeting

cxxxiii Buckingham Orthodox Monthly Meeting minutes 4th d./7th mo./1836
cxxxiv Buckingham Orthodox Monthly Meeting minutes 2nd d./10th mo./1837
cxxxv Plumstead Orthodox Preparative Meeting minutes 28th d./9th mo./1837
cxxxvi Philadelphia Yearly Meeting (Orthodox) Meeting for Sufferings 5th mo./8th d./1866

cxxxvii Buckingham Orthodox Monthly Meeting minutes 5th d./4th mo./1847
cxxxviii Matlack, p. 55

Chapter Six: Changes in Quaker Culture and Theology

cxxxix Buckingham Orthodox Monthly Meeting minutes 8th mo./5th d./1878 and November, 1878
cxl Kenderdine, p. 763
cxli One source states the date as 1893 (Inventory of Church Archives: Society of Friends, vol. 1, p. 195) and another sets the date as 1889 (Plumstead Orthodox file in Friends Historical Library)
cxlii Bronner, pp. 134-135
cxliii Frost, "Quaker Antislavery" p. 12
cxliv Powers, p. 69
cxlv Powers, p. 55
cxlvi Bronner, p. 106
cxlvii Powers, p. 57
cxlviii Bronner, p. 111
cxlix Frost, "Years" pp. 83, 100, 101
cl Brinton, p. 198
cli Caton, pp. 268–269
clii Hinshaw, p. 68
cliii Hinshaw, p. 165
cliv Brinton, pp. 199–200
clv Bronner, p. 136

Vignette: The Quaker Experience during the Civil War

clvi Philadelphia Yearly Meeting (Hicksite) Meeting for Sufferings 9th mo./18th d./1863
clvii Crothers, document available online

Chapter Seven: Plumstead Moves toward Modern Times

clviii Buckingham Hicksite Monthly Meeting minutes 11th mo./2nd d./1874
clix "Repairs Proposed" 1874
clx Buckingham Hicksite Monthly Meeting minutes 8th mo./25th d./1875
clxi Buckingham Hicksite Monthly Meeting minutes 2nd mo./7th d./1876
clxii Fell, p. 9
clxiii Historic American Buildings Survey, p. 43

clxiv Kenderdine, p. 762

clxv Buckingham Hicksite Monthly Meeting minutes 2nd mo./7th d./1887. A similar notation was made in 1891.

clxvi Buckingham Hicksite Monthly Meeting minutes 12th mo./1893 and 1st mo./1894, for example.

clxvii Philanthropic Committee, 1899

clxviii Buckingham Hicksite Monthly Meeting minutes, 2th mo./2th d./1903

clxix Kenderdine, p. 762

clxx Buckingham Hicksite Monthly Meeting minutes, 2th mo./2th d./1903

clxxi Matlack, p. 53

clxxii Buckingham Hicksite Monthly Meeting minutes, 4th mo./7th d./1902. From a report from Plumstead submitted to the Samuel Jeanes Fund requesting funds for repairs.

clxxiii Kenderdine, p. 762

clxxiv Buckingham Hicksite Monthly Meeting minutes, 4th mo./7th d./1902, 12th mo./1st d./1902, 4th mo./6th d./1903, 1st mo./4th d./1904, 5th mo./7th d./1906

clxxv Buckingham Hicksite Monthly Meeting minutes 9th mo./2nd d./1918

clxxvi Matlack, "Brief Historical Sketches" p. 122

clxxvii For example, Buckingham Hicksite Monthly Meeting minutes 11th mo./7th d./1927, 5th mo./27th d./1930, 5th mo./ 4th d./ 1931

clxxviii Buckingham Hicksite Monthly Meeting minutes 6th mo./4th d./1939

clxxix Buckingham Hicksite Monthly Meeting minutes, 4th mo./3rd d./1933 and 7th mo./2nd d./1939

clxxx Buckingham Hicksite Monthly Meeting minutes 10th mo./1st d./1933

clxxxi Buckingham Hicksite Monthly Meeting minutes 10th mo./1st d./1950

clxxxii Buckingham Hicksite Monthly Meeting minutes 4th mo./4th d./1960

clxxxiii "Milestones: Obituary of Maris Langford" 2016

clxxxiv "In 1966, Sadie Taylor, a First Day School teacher" two unpublished histories of Plumstead Meeting written by Beth Taylor

clxxxv Unpublished letters between Plumstead Worship Group, Buckingham Monthly Meeting, and Bucks Quarterly Meeting

clxxxvi Unpublished letter from Susan White, PYM recording clerk, dated June 21, 2002

clxxxvii Pennsylvania Historical Survey, p. 195

clxxxviiiCommon Schools of Pennsylvania, p. 92

clxxxix Brinton, pp. 149-151

cxc Buckingham Monthly Meeting minutes 2nd d./8th mo./1790

cxci Davis, *History,* (1876) p. 404

cxcii Buckingham Monthly Meeting minutes 2nd d./2nd mo./1807

cxciii Buckingham Monthly Meeting minutes 6th d./3rd mo./1820

cxciv Buckingham Monthly Meeting minutes 3rd d./3rd mo./1834

cxcv McNealy, p. 181

cxcvi Philadelphia Yearly Meeting minutes 1706

cxcvii Crooks, n.d.

cxcviii Buckingham Monthly Meeting Birth, Burial and Marriage Certificates 1720–1801

cxcix Michener, p. 1

cc Buckingham Monthly Meeting minutes 3rd d./12th mo./1792

cci Buckingham Monthly Meeting minutes 4th d./3rd mo./1793

ccii Buckingham Hicksite Monthly Meeting minutes December 4, 1893

cciii Kenderdine, p. 762

Walk cheerfully over the earth,
answering that of God in everyone
– George Fox